Judaism's Strange Gods

Michael A. Hoffman II

An Independent History and Research Book
Coeur d'Alene, Idaho 83816-0849

Seventh printing: February, 2005

Printed in the U.S.A.

ISBN: 0-9703784-0-8

Independent History and Research
Post Office Box 849
Coeur d'Alene, Idaho 83816

www.revisionisthistory.org

I am the Lord thy God,
thou shalt have no strange gods before me

Exodus 20: 2-3

TABLE OF CONTENTS

ILLUSTRATIONS

Preface

This writer contends in the following pages that Judaism is not the religion of the Old Testament or of the God of Israel, but rather that Judaism's gods consist of the Talmud, the Kabbalah and racial self-worship.

I further assert that Christianity is the only religion that represents the Old Testament creed of Yahweh, being the continuation and prophetic fulfillment of the Old Testament in the Gospel of the Messiah of Israel.

This book is intended for the benefit of all mankind, but due to the temporal power exerted by adherents of the ideology it unmasks, it may become a target of proscription and vilification.

I ask those who would suppress it or subject its author to obloquy, the question Paul asked of the Galatians, "Have I now become your enemy by telling you the truth?"

Michael A. Hoffman II

Part One: The Talmud

THE WEIRD cult of "Judeo-Christianity," is an oxymoron found on the lips of many Christians including even conservative ones.

This abominable "Judeo-Christianity" contrivance is of a piece with the cloning of human and animal genes or any of the other alchemical mixtures of two mutually contradictory substances which we have witnessed these last few decades in the modern cauldron.

The near-universal approbation and currency exerted by this cockamamie term exposes at one glance the level of abysmal historical ignorance which obtains today.

The Church Fathers knew of no "Judeo-Christian" tradition, since Judaism did not exist before Christ.

Before Him, there was the faith of the Israelites as it gradually decayed and was subverted by corrupt teachings such as were transmitted by the Pharisees and Sadducees.

This corruption was greatly escalated when a portion of the Israelites rejected the Messiah, Yashua (Joshua, i.e. Jesus), after which their leaders eventually made their way to Babylon, where the corrupt and reprobate, oral occult *tradition of the elders* was committed to writing and compiled as the *Mishnah,* comprising the first portion of the Talmud. At that juncture, the religion of Judaism was born.

It is the Talmud, not the Bible, which is the hermeneutic system of orthodox Judaism.

According to Robert Goldenberg, Professor of Judaic Studies at the State University of New York:

"The Talmud was *Torah.* In a paradox that determined the history of Judaism, the Talmud was Oral Torah in written form, and as such it became the clearest statement the Jew could hear of God's very word.

"...The Talmud provided the means of determining how God wanted all Jews to live, in all places, at all times. Even if the details of the law had to be altered to suit newly arisen conditions, the proper way to perform such adaptation could itself be learned from the Talmud and its commentaries...The Talmud revealed God speaking to Israel, and so the Talmud became Israel's way to God."[1]

The religion of Judaism as it has been known since it was concocted after the crucifixion of Christ is what is called "Orthodox" Judaism today.[2]

The early Church recognized Christianity as having been founded by Israelites and representing the only true religion of the Bible. It is Christians who are "a chosen generation, a royal priesthood, a holy nation..." (I Peter 2:9).

Judaism was not viewed as the repository of the spiritual truths or knowledge of the Old Testament, but as a post-Biblical, Babylonian cult totally at variance with Biblical Christianity.

---

[1] Robert Goldenberg, "Talmud," *Back to the Sources: Reading the Classic Jewish Texts* (New York: Simon and Schuster, 1984), pp. 166-167.

[2] We do not here concern ourselves with the supposed "Reform" branch of the synagogue because they do not accord the Talmud the supreme authority which Judaism does. Liberal "Reform" synagogues stand in the same relationship with Judaism as Unitarians who deny the Resurrection of Christ do with regard to Christianity: both represent a fundamental negation of the founding precepts of the religion they claim to profess. "Reform" (and in some cases "Conservative") synagogues that deny the obligations of the Talmud, do not constitute the religion of Judaism. They are ethnic and cultural offshoots. However, many liberal and secular Jews exhibit nearly the same chauvinism and racism as believers in the Talmud, by their embrace of the ideology of Zionism: "Secular...Israeli Jews hold political views and engage in rhetoric similar to that of religious Jews...For religious Jews, the blood of non-Jews has no intrinsic value; for Likud (political party of Begin, Shamir and Netanyahu) it has limited value...Most foreign observers do not realize that a sizeable segment of the Israeli Jewish public holds these chauvinistic views...The world view of Likud politicians, enthusiastically supported by followers, is basically the world view of religious Jews; it has undergone significant secularization but has kept its essential qualities." Israel Shahak and Norton Mezvinsky, *Jewish Fundamentalism in Israel,* [London: Pluto Press, 1999], pp. 11-16.

True Israelites could only be Christians, not followers of Judaism. The followers of Judaism are anti-Biblical; they had to violate the Old Testament in order to reject Jesus, for the "Scriptures testify of me."

One need only start with the historic Christian attitude toward sex and the body and contrast it with Judaism's teaching in these matters, to discover a vast and unbridgeable chasm which is nowadays obstructed and falsified in a frantic effort to appease and placate Jewish power.

Augustine, in his *Tractatus adversus Judeos* declared rabbinic Judaism to be the counterfeit of true Israel. Augustine declared that Judaism was "Israel according to the flesh," *carnal* Israel.

For Christians, the essence of the human being is the soul, for Jews it is the body, hence their worship of their own race as the type of God. [3]

Virginity is highly problematic in Judaism where defilement is defined as failure to engage in the sex act. "Anyone who does not copulate it is as if he had spilled blood." The rabbis forbid virginity. [4]

On this subject of sexuality alone it is impossible to speak of a "Judeo-Christian" tradition.

That Christ and His Gospel are betrayed by those who declare an alleged "Judeo-Christian" tradition, is of no discernible concern to the ministers, popes and pundits thus engaged. They are Jewish Pharisees in all but name, engaged in the standard modern apologetic misinterpretation of Judaism, out of "fear of the Jews"[5] and a need to ingratiate themselves with the "god of this world."

---

[3]Daniel Boyarin, "This We Know to be the Carnal Israel," *Critical Inquiry,* vol. 18, pp. 474-505; and David Biale, *Eros and the Jews,* [New York: Basic Books, 1992].

[4]Yebamot 63b. Shulhan Arukh, Even HaEzer 1:1. William Wright, *The Homilies of Aphraates, the Persian Sage* [London: 1869, vol. I, The Syriac Texts], p. 355.

[5]John: 7:13, 19:38, 20:19.

John Chrysostom: "The Jews disdained the beauty of virginity, which is not surprising since they heaped ignominy on Christ himself, who was born of a virgin" (*Homily On Virginity*).

There is no fundamental opposition between spirit and matter in Judaism. When Jesus declared in John 6 that "the flesh profiteth nothing" he was violating the oral tradition of the Pharisees:

"Rabbinic anthropology differs in this respect from...Christian-anthropology...there is not a fundamental metaphysical opposition between (body and soul)..." [6]

Judaism celebrates the body to such a sordid extent that it even has a defecation prayer which every Jewish male is commanded to recite every time he relieves himself: "Blessed art thou O Lord...who has made the human in its orifices and holes."

Everything about Judaism is either a distortion or a falsification of the Old Testament because Judaism is based on a man-made tradition that voids the Old Testament by means of a series of dispensations and loopholes.

These begin with the *Mishnah,* which represents the commitment to writing of the occult legends and lore of those Israelites who had preserved "secret knowledge" which had arisen with the worship of the golden calf, of Molech and similar abominations.

With the rejection of their Messiah and the commitment of the formerly oral traditions to writing, these Israelites completely abandoned themselves to a perversion which had once been only a persistent underground stream polluting Israel, but after Christ's crucifixion, emerged as the main ideology of those who refused to accept Jesus as their savior.

Later Talmudic rabbis styled this primary canon of written Judaism as *Mishnah* (literally "repetition"). The term signifies "oral tradition learned by constant repetition." The connotation is derived from the Hebrew denotation, the root *sh-n-y,* meaning "to repeat." Within

[6]Alon Goshen-Gottstein, *The Body as Image of God in Rabbinic Literature*, [Berkeley, Calif: 1991].

the text of the Mishnah proper, it is called *halakot,* literally, "extra-Biblical law."

Babylonian Jewish tradition in Talmud tractates Berakot 5a and Shabbat 31a teach that the *Mishnah* and the rest of the Talmud (*Gemara*) were given by God to Moses on Mt. Sinai, along with the Ten Commandments.

The *Mishnah* was completed at the end of the Second Century A.D., more than 100 years after the destruction of the second Temple by the Romans in 70 A.D. The exceptions are the tractates Sotah and Abot which are later additions misrepresented as a part of the original *Mishnah* by the rabbinic "sages" themselves (deceit compounding deceit).

Engulfed in a sea of prolix cogitations, Talmudic texts can be minefields of deception and pits of derangement and bogus reasoning, as befits those who would replace the Bible with their own authority.

Most of the laws of the religion of Judaism have no Biblical warrant; they contradict and nullify the word of God.

Where the sufficiency of Scripture is denied, the fallacies and imaginings of man come to the fore. The Talmud is one of the largest collections of such fancies and human error; sometimes intriguing and colorful, titillating the senses with the phantasmagoria of the Aggadah, but more often sordid, blasphemous and asinine, in spite of the intellectual prestige accorded its rabbinic authors.

There is a joke among those Jewish persons (*frierim*) who might be described as resentful and reluctant "Jews" -- those who are regularly swindled by the rabbis, by the *kashrut* (kosher food) racket and oppressed by the multiple other forms of fraud and thinly veiled taxation foisted on them by their watchdogs and masters.

This joke ridicules the fact that so much of Jewish law, from the burden of keeping a separate kitchen for meat and dairy products, to the wearing of the ever-present head covering for men, is not of God, but derived from man-made tradition.

The joke is related herein because it illustrates rather well the type of Talmudic "reasoning" that became authoritative when the Pharisaic party rejected Israel's Messiah, and formally codified the anti-Scriptural precepts of the elders, by committing them to writing as the basis of the novel religion of Judaism, as opposed to the exclusively Old Testament foundations of Christian Israel.

The joke is occasioned by the bitterness of the *frierim* toward the judicial decision of Rabbi Joseph Karo, who imposed taxation on them for the support of indolent "Talmud students," including married men who sometimes spend a lifetime loitering in a kollel. The esteemed Halakhic codifier Karo had over-ruled that other giant of Jewish jurisprudence, his medieval predecessor, Moses Maimonides.

Maimonides had decreed that Talmud students should work at least nominally, since this was the practice of the important early Pharisee, Hillel the Elder. But Karo decided that Talmud students do not have to engage in work and can be supported by taxes. Karo said that "we must assume that he (Hillel) engaged in labor only at the beginning of his studies...How can we assume that when Hillel became famous the people did not give him support?" [7]

It is not difficult to see that Rabbi Karo has drawn his assumption from thin air.

To underscore the arbitrary nature of these out-in-the-ozone rabbinic rulings, the joke has it that a man quits Judaism and the first thing he does is remove his *kippah,* or skullcap. A rabbi challenges him to put it back on, but the disgruntled man replies that the rabbi will first have to furnish proof from the Bible that a head-covering for men is required.

The rabbi in the joke answers: "The Bible says: 'And Abraham went--' (to some destination). Can you imagine that he went without a head-covering?"

The rabbi's "reasoning" via his own imagination is very familiar to those acquainted with the works of Karo, Rambam, Rashi and Hillel, to say nothing of the *oeuvre* of

---

[7] Rabbi Joseh Karo, *Kesef Mishne.* Karo's ruling is still in effect and Israeli Talmud students are supported by a type of welfare.

the Gentile-hating mystagogues of the Kabbalah, such as Isaac Luria, Nachman of Bratslav and Shneur Zalman of Lyady.

A common rabbinic defense against criticism of the more blatantly horrible passages in the Talmud, is the allegation that the Talmud is merely a record of debates (*mahloket*) between *tanna'im* and *amora'm*[8] and that by seizing on one portion of the controversy and upholding that passage as authoritative, the critic errs, for no Talmudic sanction is given to either side of the debate in Talmud.

This is disingenuous, since the Mishnah and key Talmudic amplifications of it, comprise dogmatic Jewish law (*halakhah*) by which every believing orthodox Jewish person is enslaved down to the most minute and intimate particulars of his or her daily life.

How Talmudic law is deduced and adjudicated is often a mystery to the non-Judaic mentality, but that it constitutes *halakhah* is undeniable.

The key point here is that the appearance of Talmudic indeterminacy does not preclude law-making by majority rabbinical consensus, which is the process by which Talmudic law is formed, both in terms of the decision on what constituted the oral law of the elders as presented in the Mishnah (*halakhah lemosheh misinai*), as well as the subsequent *Mitzvot derabanan* (rabbinical commandments) found in the Gemara, arising from the deductive process known as *Midot shehatorah nidreshet bahen.*

As a public relations ploy, certain rabbis and Judaic leaders pretend otherwise, revealing the low opinion they have of the public, whom they believe will swallow the

---

[8]The categories of *Tanna'im* ("repeaters") and *amora'm* ("interpreters") represent two rabbinic eras. The *Tanna'im* consisted of the elders of the oral tradition: Hillel the Elder, Gamaliel the Elder, Shammai, Zaddok, Eliezer and other first and second century A.D. Pharisees who kept alive their tradition by repeating it and eventually forming it into the Mishnah. The *amora'm* come after the Mishnah, and their amplification of it forms the teaching of a later period of Talmud, called Gemara.

line about the Talmud being a mere book of debates, where no clear teaching or law-making emerges, even though this claim is demonstrably false.

The cunning intent behind the deliberate sowing of this misapprehension rests in the stratagem that by promoting the idea that the Talmud is a collection of disputes meaning everything and nothing, no indictment of the Talmud is possible, since another text can always be cited to contradict the offending one.

But in practice the investigator need only examine the historic discipline and practice of Judaism from its codification after the crucifixion of Jesus to the rise of liberal-apostate Jewish groups during the 18th century European Enlightenment, to ascertain that a body of law codified in the Talmud exerted the most profound command over individual Jews and governs their behavior.

Following the trail of that body of law begins with linking it to the corresponding orthodox Jewish practice that has arisen from it. By this means we discern the synthesis of seemingly opposing tendencies that forms the Talmudic dialectic.

For example, while it can be accurately said that orthodox Judaism consists in living a life for this world through the body, the means by which this living is implemented are psychotic.

Sexuality in orthodox Judaism is mediated by thousands of regulations, because Talmud is the essence of the bureaucratic mentality, a fact that emerges as America and Britain abandon Christian-Israel's Biblically-inspired Anglo-Saxon jurisprudence and Common Law and embrace the Talmudic law of Big Brother bureaucracy.

The American system of jurisprudence has degenerated from courts that ruled according to God's law, to courts that *make the law* through judicial interpretation and case law (precedent). The latter is entirely Talmudic and reflects the subversion of our nation:

"The growth of Talmudic Law, in all its aspects, was for the most part, the work of judicial interpretation rather than of formal legislation...The judge served in effect as a creator of law and not only as its interpreter..." [9]

To better investigate the root of the confusion about Judaism, let us now examine a classic statement of modern Protestantism's view of Judaism, as presented by conservative Presbyterian theologian Douglas Jones:

"...consider the case of Abraham, that ancient father of Judaism and Christianity...One of the best ways of beginning to think about the nature of Christianity is to think of it in the light of Judaism.

"Today, we so often think of Judaism and Christianity as two distinct religions, almost like Buddhism and Islam. But early Christianity never saw itself in that way. The earliest Christians saw themselves as faithful Jews simply following Jewish teachings. In fact, the first main dispute in the Christian church was whether non-Jews, the Gentiles, could even be a part of Christianity!

"Christianity self-consciously saw itself as the continuing outgrowth, the fulfillment, of true Judaism. As such, Christianity didn't start in the first century but long before with King David, Moses, Abraham, and ultimately the first man, Adam. Everything in older Judaism was building up and pointing to the work of Jesus Christ. Over and over, the early disciples explained that Christ was the fulfillment of the ancient promises of Judaism.

"...So when we start thinking about Christianity, we have to understand its very Jewish roots. We should assume that Christianity ought to look and sound like Judaism except when it explicitly claims to change something. We should expect that the Scriptures, institutions, basic principles, laws, meditations, family life, etc. of Judaism would carry over into Christianity, unless Christ, the final prophet, authoritatively changed a practice....Christianity's Jewishness is pervasive indeed." [10]

By improper application of the words Jew and Judaism, the preceding statement of modern conservative

[9]Rabbi Ben Zion Bokser, *The Wisdom of the Talmud* [New York: Philosophical Library, 1951). Thanks to Earl F. Jones of Deming, New Mexico for bringing this to my attention.

[10] "Why & What: A Brief Introduction to Christianity" by Rev. Douglas Jones, The Canon Press, [www.canonpress.org/whywhat.htm]. Mr. Jones is senior editor of the orthodox Presbyterian magazine, *Credenda Agenda*.

Protestantism's view of Judaism, extols a palimpsest of confusion.

First and foremost, by terming the Old Testament religion of Yahwehism as "Judaism" an inevitable and inexorable connection is established between the religion of those who rejected Jesus as the Messiah, and the Old Testament religion of His Father, Yahweh.

The reader is given the distinct impression that modern Judaism bears within it the seeds of the religion of the Old Testament, that it is the Old Testament religion without Christ.

Nothing could be further from the truth. Nothing could be a greater source of delusion. To ascribe to the ancient Israelite religion the term "Judaism" is a grave lexical and hermeneutic error.

It gives to the creed of the entire Twelve Tribes of Israel and their Covenant Elohim, the title of a perverse man-made tradition that flourished among one segment of the offspring of the fourth son of the patriarch Jacob (the tribe of Judah).

The word "Jew" is a corrupted form of the word Judah. It is a reference to two of the 12 tribes of Israel, Judah and Benjamin, and does not even appear in the Bible until II Kings 16:6 and then again in 25:25 and II Chronicles 32:18.

Paul's allusion to the "Jews' religion" in this context is instructive. Paul's reference in this regard is negative: "And profited in the Jews' religion above many my equals in mine own nation, being more exceedingly zealous of the traditions of my fathers." (Galatians 1:14).

The hallmarks of the "Jews' religion" according to Paul, are two-fold: persecution of God's Church (I Thessalonians 2:14-16), and allegiance to the "traditions" of men.

The Pharisees asked Jesus why His followers disobeyed the Talmud (at that time known as the "tradition of the elders" and not yet in written form), by refusing to engage in *ritual* hand-washing: "Why do thy disciples transgress the tradition of the elders? For they wash not their hands when they eat bread."

"But Jesus said unto them, 'Why do ye transgress the

commandment of God by your tradition?" (Matthew 15: 2-3).

How can it be said that "Judaism" (the "Jews' religion") is the root of Christianity, when according to Paul, it is a religion of man-made traditions and according to Jesus Christ, Judaism's traditions of men made the Law of Yahweh of "none effect"? (Matthew 15:9).

How can it be said that "Judaism" is the root of Christianity, when in the Old Testament there was no "Judaism"? One searches in vain for the term, yet modernist Christians today use it almost exclusively to describe the religion of the Old Testament, of Yahweh and His people.

After some Jews rejected their Messiah they formalized the tradition of the elders condemned by Christ as the very nullification of the Law of God, and that *new religion* is accurately and properly termed Judaism:

"This new system, treated at first as simply provisional because of the surviving hope of restoring the Jewish commonwealth, had soon to be accepted as definitive...Then it was that Rabbinical or Talmudical Judaism fully asserted its authority...the Mishna 'Oral Teaching' completed by Rabbi Juda I, committed ultimately to writing in the form of the Jerusalem and Babylonian Talmuds and expounded by generations of teachers in the schools of Palestine and Babylonia, held undisputed sway over the minds and consciences of the Jews.

"In fact, this long acceptation of the Talmud by the Jewish race, before its center shifted from the East to the West, so impressed this...Law (Mishnah) upon the hearts of the Jews that down to the present day Judaism has remained essentially Talmudical both in its theory and in its practice...Orthodox Judaism...distinctly admits the absolutely binding force of the oral Law..." [11]

Judaism has as its god, not Yahweh, but the Jewish people, whose self-worship is at the core of the Talmud.

It has as its law, not the Tanakh (books of the Old Testament), but the Talmud.

---

[11]*The Catholic Encyclopedia* (New York: Robert Appleton Co., 1912), vol. 8, p. 402.

Jesus proclaimed that the initial stage of Talmud, the Mishnah, which existed in its oral form in Christ's time -- was *the tradition of the elders* which nullifies the word of God:

"Then came together unto him the Pharisees and certain of the scribes which came from Jerusalem, gathered around Jesus and saw some of his disciples eating food with "unclean" -- that is, ceremonially unwashed -- hands, and they found fault.

"For the Pharisees, and all the Jews, do not eat unless they give their hands a ceremonial washing, holding to the tradition of the elders. And when they come from the marketplace, unless they wash, they do not eat. And they observe many other traditions, such as the washing of cups, pitchers and kettles.

"Then the Pharisees and scribes asked Jesus, 'Why do your disciples not live according to the traditions of the elders, instead of eating their food with 'unclean' hands?

"He answered and said unto them, "Well hath Isaiah prophesied of you hypocrites, as it is written, 'This people honors me with their lips but their heart is far from me.'

"How be it in vain do they worship me, teaching for doctrine the commandments of men.

"For laying aside the commandments of God you observe your own traditions. You reject the commandment of God that you may keep your own tradition.

"For Moses gave you this law from God: 'Honor thy father and thy mother' and 'Anyone who curses his father or mother must be put to death.' But you say that a man may say to his father or mother, 'I can't help you, for I have vowed to give to God what I could have given to you.' You let him disregard his father or his mother.

"Thus you make the word of God of none effect by your tradition that you have handed down." [12]

---

[12]Mark 7:1-13. The issue here is not God's laws of hygiene for prevention of insanitary conditions, but burdensome and useless, ritual purification based on man-made additions to God's laws. The Talmud extols filth. Being soiled by feces and urine for example, is not regarded as defilement by the Talmud. Cf. Judith R. Wegner, *Chattel or Person: The Status of Women in the Mishnah* [NY: Oxford U. Press, 1988], f. 251 on p. 242. Jesus alludes to the hypocritical effects of such rituals in Matthew 23:25-26.

Here, as in Matthew 15: 1-9, is direct and incontrovertible refutation in the Gospel of Jesus Christ of the falsification inherent in the Oral Law and its traditions, which the Pharisees and their heirs mendaciously claimed was a secret teaching from Moses.

Jesus contrasts the Law of God as Moses actually gave it with the nullification of that law by adherence to the tradition of the elders, which would soon be committed to writing, forming the Mishnah and the rest of the Talmud and upon which the religion of Judaism would be based.

Yet Christ's admonition was not heeded by the Pharisaic leadership and an entire religion of hypocrisy would subsequently arise, founded upon these "traditions of the elders," and their Talmudic counterfeit of God's word; all performed in the name of God, His Word and of Israel.

Jewish theologians claim that "...ancient rabbis taught that the revelation granted to Moses had been delivered in two forms, a smaller revelation in writing and the larger one kept oral. This 'Oral Torah' had been transmitted faithfully by the leaders of each generation to their successors, by Moses to Joshua, and then to the elders, then to the prophets, to the men of the Great Assembly, to the leaders of the Pharisees, and finally to the earliest rabbis. The earliest rabbis saw themselves, as noted, as heirs to the Pharisees." [13]

This supposed transmission of the "Oral Torah," the tradition of the elders, from Moses to Joshua, to the prophets, was challenged by Jesus Christ who termed it not Torah, but the commandments of men which nullify the word and doctrine of God, making the tale of the transmission itself a fraud.

It is a lie concocted in hell to claim Moses issued two sets of laws, one written and public, the other an oral tradition that was secret. In all of the Bible there is nothing to support this imposture. This diabolic fantasy is the basis of the religion of Judaism, and it this institutionalized, dogmatic delusion which distinguishes Judaism from the

---

[13]Robert Goldenberg, op. cit., p. 130.

only Bible-based faith -- Christianity -- representing as it does the continuation of the Old Testament religion of Israel as it finds its prophetic fulfillment in the Gospel of the Messiah of Israel.

The spurious claim of an oral tradition of the elders bequeathed by God to Moses, is anti-Biblical and it was denounced by Jesus Christ Himself. In the divine brilliance of Jesus upon which the cunning and cleverness of the Pharisees was turned against them time and again, Jesus very simply and forthrightly illuminated the fact that if the Pharisees' tradition had been from Moses, then the Pharisees would have become Christians:

"For had ye believed Moses, ye would have believed me, for he wrote of me. But if ye believe not his writings, how shall ye believe my words?" (John 5: 46-47).

Christ has just annihilated, in one paragraph, the basis for the religion of Judaism and its conceit of a tradition given to it by Moses, for had such a tradition existed it would have testified of Jesus.

Instead, He tells them point-blank that they don't believe Moses. Jesus crushed the whole beguiling system of indoctrination predicated on the Pharisaic myth of a divinely-inspired, oral tradition of the elders.[14]

The French historian Daniel-Rops, in his seminal study of Christ and the early Church, writes:

"From the Talmudic definition of various ritual observances we can see how well justified were the sarcasms of Jesus; for instance it was forbidden to eat on the Sabbath day an egg of which the greater part had been laid by a hen before a second star was visible in the sky. On the sacred day it was as much a crime to crush a flea as to

---

[14]The response of last resort to these facts is to rehabilitate the Pharisees and cast doubt on the New Testament account of Christ's ministry. The establishment now promotes the view that the Pharisees were misunderstood victims of four bigoted evangelists and two mendacious apostles; Judas was a scapegoat and Jesus Himself was confused and His Resurrection merely "symbolic." This is the revised life of Christ as put forth by the "Jesus Seminar" and similar Talmudic front-groups.

kill a camel, although Rabbi Abba Saul conceded that one might gently squeeze the flea and Rabbi Zamuel very broadmindedly allowed one to cut off its feet...

"We can also see, in these rabbinical texts, their immeasurable contempt for the common people, the peasants, the *am-ha-arez,* who did not enjoy the privilege of knowing the Law. And we can understand how the Gospel, sown among these untouchables, yielded such an immediate and mighty harvest." [15]

The Pharisaic condemnation of the Israelite peasant class may be found in John 7:48-49: "Is there a single one of us rulers or Pharisees who believes in him (Jesus)? No! But only this people that knoweth not the Law and are accursed."

Israelite peasants were "regarded...as louts sunk in ritual impurity," and the Pharisee leader Hillel viewed them as sub-human: "a churl without a conscience." [16]

According to the article titled "Am-ha-erez" by S. Bialoblotzki in the *Jewish Encyclopedia,* the common people of Israel "encountered only the most brutal repulsion" from the Pharisees, but when they became Christians they found "welcome and affection."

Persecution of Christian Israelites by Pharisees of the first century entails not only the crucifixion of Jesus but other murders, the most notorious being the stoning of Stephen, the attempted murder of Paul and, according to Josephus, the judicial murder of James the Just in the absence of the Roman governor.[17]

Judaism is a poisonous counterfeit, a "synagogue of Satan" (Rev. 2:9). To make any connection between a religion

---

[15]Daniel-Rops, *Jesus and His Times,* translated from the French by Ruby Millar [Garden City, NY: Image Books, 1958], pp. 67-68.

[16]Ibid., p. 157.

[17]In *The Decline and Fall of the Roman Empire,* historian Edward Gibbon records little known massacres perpetrated by Jews against Gentiles in the first centuries A.D. in Egypt, Cyprus and Cyrene. See chapters 16 and 78.

which directly contradicts Jesus Christ's own solemn, admonitory condemnation of man-made traditions, and the religion of the God of Israel, is not only irrational and unscriptural, but an abomination.

If Judaism were simply -- having rejected Christ -- a corrupted variant of the ancient religion of the Israelites, then Judaism would not have, over the centuries, despised, reviled, denounced, persecuted, beaten and murdered the Karaites.

Paul Johnson in his *History of the Jews* recounts how, in the 1100s, in the walled Jewish ghetto in Constantinople there was an interior wall that separated the thousands of followers of the religion of Judaism and its Talmud from five hundred anti-Talmudic, Bible-only Karaites. [18]

The Karaites are a tiny Jewish sect which attempts to understand and follow the Old Testament without either the Talmud or Jesus: "...as early as the eighth century of our era the authority of the Talmud was denied in favor of Biblical supremacy by the sect of the Karaites." [19]

Yet the Karaites are hated and severely persecuted by the adherents of Judaism. Why?

Because Judaism is Talmudism, not Old Testament, and those who revere the Old Testament teachings outside the prism of Talmud are its hereditary enemies.

A counterfeit cannot be said to be the heir to a genuine article. Judaism, whether qualified as ancient or not, is totally alien to the only Biblical religion on earth today, Christianity.

The religion of the God of Israel is Christianity. It has no root in the religion of Judaism which is the religion of

---

[18]According to Prof. Albert S. Lindemann of the University of California at Santa Barbara, the Karaites are "...an ancient dissident Jewish sect that did not recognize the Talmud. A few thousand of its followers survived in the Caucasus area..the tsarist regime recognized this distinctness and did not apply anti-Jewish legislation to them." *Esau's Tears: Modern Anti-Semitism and the Rise of the Jews* [NY: Cambridge Univ. Press, 1997], pp. 430-431.

[19]*Catholic Encyclopedia,* op. cit.

the Talmud.

Judaism is not simply a perversion, to some degree or other, of God's original revelation to the Hebrew nation. It is the very religion of nullification of the Old Testament; a diabolic counterfeit. Now, what fellowship hath darkness with light? None.

When Mr. Jones states, "Christianity ought to look and sound like Judaism except when it explicitly claims to change something," he is, no doubt unconsciously and with good intentions, creating a link in the minds of Christians between those observances practiced by Talmudic rabbis today and the ancient religion of Israel.

This is the fatal flaw in modern Christianity. They pay some obeisance, whether small or great, to the heinous hoax that there is a Biblical root to Judaism.

Can it be said that Christians who convert to Voodoo have a Christian root? Should we sit at the feet of formerly Christian Voodoo practitioners in order to gain insight into the Early Church?

Do the followers of Christ who betray Him to follow strange gods, be they Pan, Zoroaster or Voodoo, offer us some resonance of Christian heritage to which we must pay honor or study?

The answer is a resounding no. These people turned their backs on their solemn *vocavo,* their calling from God Himself. Heeding them in any way, except as wretched failures to be pitied and prayed for, is a recipe for disaster.

The Israelites who apostasized to follow the new religion of Judaism and its strange gods -- Talmud, Kabbalah and self-worship -- have no more claim on us than any other idol-worshipper.

Strange Qualifications for Biblical Expertise

Roman Catholic Books of Fort Collins, Colorado is the publishing arm of a Catholic organization that clings to the old Latin Tridentine Mass *and* the Pope of Rome (as opposed to the growing corps of Tridentine Catholics who regard the Pope as a public heretic and believe the "See of Peter" is vacant, i.e. *sede vacantist*).

In the spring of 2000, a four-page catalog of selections

from the Roman Catholic Books company appeared as an insert in the flagship papist newspaper, *The Wanderer*. One of the items advertised in the catalog was a reprint of *The Nazarene,* a book by Israel "Eugenio" Zolli, the former chief rabbi of Rome, who converted to Catholicism. [20]

In recommending the volume, Roman Catholic Books stated: "The years Zolli devoted to learning ancient languages and studying the Torah, Talmud, Midrash and other sacred Jewish texts gave him an advantage over Christian scholars. They came to Hebraic literature as outsiders; but Zolli had lived and breathed the words of the prophets and rabbis all his life. For this reason, Zolli's book stands head and shoulders above the innumerable Biblical commentaries."

In this advertisement for Zolli's book we observe the calamitous notion that there is some kernel of Biblical heritage worthy of our approbation and study in Judaism, which has contradicted and rejected Yahweh's teaching and laws.

The predominance of the faulty idea that Judaism is the root of Christianity, is responsible for much of the paralysis and impotence in the Church today.

Prof. Israel Shahak of Hebrew University, Jerusalem, and Prof. Norton Mezvinsky of Connecticut State University write:

"The Bible anyway is not the book that primarily determines the practices and doctrines of Orthodox Jews. The most fundamentalist Orthodox Jews are largely ignorant of major parts of the Bible and know some parts only through commentaries that distort

---

[20]The story of Rabbi Zolli has been blacked out by the establishment who seek to tar Pius XII with a Nazi stigma. As Chief Rabbi of Rome during WWII, Zolli was able to judge Pius XII's actions under the Nazi occupation first hand. So impressed was this rabbi with the pope's rescue effort on behalf of Italy's Jewish population, that Rabbi Zolli converted to Catholicism in 1945 and changed his name from Israel to Eugenio in honor of the pope (Pius XII was christened Eugenio, his surname was Pacelli). Zolli died in 1956.

meaning...Judaism, as it came to be known, did not exist during the biblical period." [21]

Roman Catholic Books does not seem to grasp the fact that no other religion prepares one for the study, and more importantly the true understanding of the Bible than Christianity.

It is one thing to suggest that a lifelong facility with Hebrew is a significant aid to Bible exegesis. One may obtain such facility through diligent language study from an early age, so the advantage is not one of religion but of precocity and pedagogy.

It is quite another matter however, to claim that immersion in the Talmud and Midrash gives a Jewish scholar a theological advantage over Christian scholars who base their study of God's Word solely on the Old and New Testament and the Early Church. To make such a claim is to actually say that being familiar with a huge compendium of the lies and fantasies of men is an advantage over a researcher who has hewed to God's Word, and to the scholarship of those Christian exegetes who expound the Bible in faithful submission to its divine authority.

Like the Talmud, the Midrash upholds the rabbinic fallacy that the Bible is deficient and incomplete; that it requires the intervention of Midrashic traditions concocted between 400 and 1200 A.D. to be understood.

Barry W. Holtz, Professor at the Jewish Theological Seminary of America and director of the seminary's Melton Research Center states:

"The Bible is loath to tell us the motivations, feelings, or thoughts of characters. Rarely giving us descriptive details either of people or places, it is composed in a stark, uncompromising style. Hence, in the laconic style of the Bible, we find one significant cause of the necessity of Midrash.

"Midrash comes to fill the gaps, to tell us the details the Bible teasingly leaves out: what did Isaac think as his father took him to be sacrificed? The Bible doesn't tell us, but Midrash fills it in with

[21]Israel Shahak and Norton Mezvinsky, *Jewish Fundamentalism in Israel* [op. cit.], p. 2.

rich and varied descriptions.

"Why did Cain kill Abel? Once again the Bible is silent, but Midrash is filled with explanation. How tall was Adam when he walked in the Garden?

"Look to the midrashic materials, not the Bible for such details...

"Where the Bible is mysterious and silent, Midrash comes to unravel the mystery.

"...the Bible often states matters of law without clarification or detail...Observant Jews today keep separate dishes for milk and meat, but where is that outlined in the Bible? Nowhere in fact. It was the Midrash of rabbinic Judaism, legal Midrash, that defined the laws."[22]

The Catholic publishing company that recommends Zolli's book because the author steeped himself for decades in the impostures and charlantry of rabbinic tradition, can only be ignorant of the actual character and content of the Talmud and the Midrash.

Presbyterian theologian Douglas Jones associates ancient Israel with Judaism, further compounding the oxymoronic myth of a Judeo-Christian tradition. For modern Protestantism to announce that Abraham is the father of Judaism *and* Christianity is to proclaim him the father of the Pharisees, and their tradition of the elders, contradicting the very heart of what Jesus proclaimed to the Pharisees in the book of John, chapter 8.

According to the Oxford English Dictionary, Christendom existed for 1494 years before this term Judaism was even coined in English, yet modernist Christians assign this name to the ancient Israelite religion of Yahweh.

"Well, okay, so what?" might be the sloppy, slothful modern reply. "It's just a word." But as William N. Grimstad states in his magisterial work, *Talk About Hate,* "We need to get to the bottom of the fact that ninety percent of what is haywire...has to do not with water pollution or air pollution but with *word* pollution."

Indeed, the misuse of words in this digital media/infotainment age has repercussions far beyond the

----

[22] Barry W. Holtz, "Midrash," *Back to the Sources: Reading the Classic Jewish Texts,* (op. cit.), pp. 180-181.

realm of the academic. Precision is of crucial importance and the failure to select the accurate word or term for a thing can mislead whole nations for generations. The substitution of Judaism for Israelite is perhaps one of the most spectacular examples of this detrimental process in action.

Let us say, for the sake of argument, that Presbyterian leader Jones had written, "Today, we so often think of the Israelites and the Christians as two distinct religions, almost like Buddhism and Islam. But early Christianity never saw itself in that way. The earliest Christians saw themselves as faithful Israelites simply following Yahweh's teachings. In fact, the first main dispute in the Christian church was whether non-Israelites, the Gentiles, could even be a part of Christianity!"

Had Jones written the preceding there would be no argument, because the names Israelite and Yahweh are direct and historically accurate representations of the people, beliefs and deity of the Old Testament creed.

In fact, these accurate descriptive terms were in general use by Christian writers, scholars and theologians for centuries before the dawn of the modern period and the commensurate enormous pressure on the Church to pay homage to counterfeit Israel--*carnal Israel*, to use Augustine's term--a religion of ever-increasing dead ritual and occult superstition from the first century A.D. onward.

According to one of the leading orthodox rabbis and Jewish scholars in America, Jacob Neusner:

"This book introduces the structure and the functioning system of Rabbinic Judaism...the particular religious system set forth by sages, or 'rabbis' who flourished in the first six centuries C.E. This same Judaism is also called 'talmudic' because its main statement is set forth by the Talmud of Babylonia..." [23]

Rabbi Neusner refers to a "Rabbinic Judaism." He indicates that it arose in Babylon during the centuries

---

[23] Jacob Neusner, *Rabbinic Judaism: Structure and System* (Minneapolis, Minnesota: Augsburg Fortress, 1995), p. vii.

after Christ was crucified.

Rabbi Neusner further notes that "rabbinic literature took shape during the nascent and formative age of Christianity."

He calls Christianity: "...a challenge that had to be met, for Christianity appealed to the same authoritative writings, the Hebrew scriptures of ancient Israel, that this Judaism formulated in its way."[24]

Notice the delineation Neusner makes between the ancient Hebrew scriptures and the rabbinic literature. They are quite patently not the same! The former is the ancient root of Christianity. The latter, formulated after Christ's incarnation and crucifixion, is the modern root of Judaism.

A Closer Look at "Rabbinic Literature"

Let us take a closer look at this formative "rabbinic literature." It is formative because it, and not the Old Testament, is the foundation stone of Judaism.

The tradition of the elders condemned by Christ in Mark 7 and Matthew 15 was an oral gnosis that preserved the thinking behind the idolatry and the apostasy of the Israelites who had worshipped the Golden calf and fed their children to Molech.

It was an undercurrent of corruption ever-threatening to boil upward and become institutionalized into a formal and competing religion, by being committed to writing.

The boiling point of corruption was reached after the Pharisaic Jewish leadership rejected the Messiah.

Having rejected the Biblical Messiah, they were guilty of having perpetrated an enormous, indeed a cosmic crime against God's law, His prophecies and prophets.

As a result of the corrupting effects of this epochal transgression, they began to commit their oral traditions to writing, beginning with the Mishnah.

Rabbi Neusner admits that: "The Mishnah certainly is the first document of rabbinic Judaism. Formally, it stands at the center of the system, since the principal subsequent rabbinic documents, the Talmuds, lay themselves out as if

---

[24]Ibid., p. viii.

they were exegeses of Mishnah..."[25]

Not the Book of Genesis, not the Pentateuch, but the Mishnah is the "first document" of Judaism, standing at the "center of the system." How can it be said that Judaism represents the teaching of Moses, when the Bible is not the center of the system? Is this what Moses taught?

It may come as a shock to learn that the rabbis are conscious of their monumental fraud and they privately admit among themselves that their system has no basis in Moses. In a cryptic passage from a book of the Jewish Kabbalah (Tikkunei Zohar 1:27b), buried within a double-entendre, is a reference to the Mishnah actually being "the burial place of Moses." How has our understanding of Judaism been so fundamentally distorted? How has so great a fraud been perpetrated as the claim that Judaism is based on the Bible, when Judaism actually *began* with the Talmud of Babylon?

Part of the answer may be found in the fact that Judaism began to infiltrate the Roman Catholic Church in earnest and contributed as well to the rise of certain major denominations of Protestantism, thanks to a myth which gained cachet during the Renaissance. The nature of this deliberately-planted disinformation was that the religion of Judaism was the Biblical religion *par excellence* and that for a Christian intellectual or spiritual seeker to truly know the Old Testament it was necessary to in some degree consult a rabbi. [26]

---

[25] Ibid., p. 22.

[26] The occult infiltration of the Church was well under way by the 15th century when the hermetic, Neo-Platonic school of so-called "Christian Kabbalists" led by Pico della Mirandola, circulated the Kabbalistic theses in Rome, whose central theme was that "No science can better convince us of the divinity of Christ than magic and Kabbalah." Rabbi Ben Zion Bokser claims that "Pope Sixtus IV was so delighted with his (Pico's) work that he urged him to translate Cabbalistic texts into Latin for the use of divinity students" (*The Maharal*, 1994, p. 11). Pico was followed in 1517 by Johannes Reuchlin whose *De Arte Cabalistica* put gematria (a Jewish numerological system), to

In modern times, the hysteria whipped up around the concepts of "anti-semitism" and "The Holocaust," caused frightened and guilt-laden Gentiles and Christians to halt almost all critical inquiry into the thesis that Judaism is synonymous with the Old Testament.

To view the thesis with skepticism became another thought-crime, another exercise in heinous "anti-semitism" that would of course, inevitably lead to another "Holocaust."

By this impressively effective intimidation device, the hoax that Judaism was *the* Biblical religion, was validated and given near-universal cachet.

But scared rabbits do not make for good scholars or good Christians, as William Scott Green of the University of Rochester, a contributor to Rabbi Neusner's *Rabbinic Judaism* book, makes plain:

"It is commonplace to classify Rabbinic Judaism as a...religion in which practice and belief derive from the study and interpretation of Scripture...The...model depicts Rabbinic Judaism as an...exegetical development out of Scripture itself...The model makes reading and interpreting the Bible the quintessential rabbinic activities...

"Rabbinic Judaism emerges as Bible-centered--the Bible read, the Bible studied, the Bible interpreted, the Bible 'put into practice'...Indeed the picture of...rabbis as Bible readers expounding their religion out of Scripture has a powerful intuitive plausibility in a culture in which religion is conceived largely in Protestant terms..."

But, the "model...blocks our perception of the particularities of rabbinic culture...the rabbis' interest in Scripture was hardly comprehensive, and vast segments of it, including much of prophecy and the Deuteronomic history, escaped their interpretation...

"Scripture neither determined the agenda nor provided the ubiquitous focus of rabbinic literary activity and

use in Bible study; by the Franciscan monk Francesco Giorgi's 1525 tribute to the Zohar, *De Harmonia mundi* and Cornelius Agrippa's *De Occulta Philosophia* of 1531; all these culminated in the 1564 occult masterwork, *Monas hieroglyphica* by the reigning figure of Protestant occultism, the mathematician Dr. John "007" Dee, astrologer royal to Queen Elizabeth I and the founder of Freemasonry.

imagination...substantial portions of rabbinic teaching--for example, on matters as basic and important as Sabbath observance--have scant Scriptural support.

"(The) complex of rabbinically ordained practices...including most of the rules for the treatment of Scripture itself--do not derive from Scripture at all. Rabbinism's initial concern was the elaboration and refinement of its own system. Attaching the system to Scripture was secondary. It therefore is misleading to depict Rabbinic Judaism primarily as the consequence of an exegetical process or the organic unfolding of Scripture. Rather, rabbinism began as the work of a small, ambitious, and homogenous group of pseudo-priests...

"By the third century, (A.D.) the rabbis expressed their self-conception in the ideology of 'oral Torah,' which held that a comprehensive body of teachings and practices (*halakot*) not included in Scripture had been given by God and through Moses only to the rabbinic establishment." [27]

Green gives the origin of Judaism as 70 A.D (although he substitutes for the word Judaism the word rabbinism): "...it helps to remember that rabbinism's initial catalyst was neither the canonization of the Hebrew Bible nor readerly research of Scripture but the demise of the Second Temple...[28]

Judaism is the product of a "small, ambitious, and homogenous group of pseudo-priests..." The Talmud, beginning with the Mishnah, is the chief Scripture of the religion of Judaism. The great, Pharisaic "sages of blessed memory" decree this themselves in the Talmud.

From the Talmud, Shabbat 15c and Baba Metzia 33A, comes the three propositions of the revered, Gentile-hating Rabbi Shimon ben Yohai, one of the most honored of all Jewish "sages" whose supposed burial site in the Israeli state is the scene of a huge, annual mass pilgrimage. Yohai wrote:

A. "He who occupies himself with Scripture gains merit that is no merit.

---

[27] *Rabbinic Judaism* by Jacob Neusner with a contribution by William Scott Green, pp. 31-34, (op. cit.).

[28] Ibid., p. 33.

B. "He who occupies himself with Mishnah gains merit for which people receive a reward.

C. "He who occupies himself with Talmud--there is no source of merit greater than this."

What part of the preceding unimpeachable statement from the supreme holy book of Judaism do Gentiles and Christians not understand?

Old Testament study is denigrated in Judaism unless it is viewed through the distorting prism of Talmud. This is what Jesus Christ stated in Mark chapter 7 about the oral tradition of the elders that became the Talmud when it was written down, it makes the Bible of "none effect."

Judaism is the religion of the tradition of the elders and the nullification of the Old Testament, exactly as Jesus Christ stated, yet his bold words of truth are so politically incorrect in our current Jewish age that, "for fear of the Jews," every somersault must be turned by those who claim to be His followers today, in order to blot out Christ's own words of warning, and conform instead to the iron dogma that the adherents of Judaism are the "People of the Book."

Indeed they are, but that book is not the Old Testament Scriptures, it is the Babylonian Talmud.

Dead Ritual Fetish: The Torah Scrolls

Now the reader may ask, "But what of the Torah scrolls carried through the synagogues with such extreme reverence?"

Well, what of it? Every idolater reverences his totem-pole, but the worship of a dead thing does not give it life. The mutilated *"sefer Torah"* scrolls carried in the pagan synagogue rites, contain no vowels. The scrolls are composed entirely in consonants. These scrolls are almost unreadable and virtually meaningless.

They are reverenced by these Jewish pagans as holy relics, as false gods in a substitution game. Yahweh destroyed the Temple and took away the Holy of Holies-- which was rent at Christ's crucifixion.

They had nowhere Biblically authentic to turn, except toward Jesus Christ, but they refused Him, and in their perversity they invented the religion of Judaism and established the idolatry of the scrolls as a substitute for the Temple and the Holy of Holies.

Because the scrolls cannot be read and do not derive their sacred status from their textual intelligibility, but as physical artifacts to be worshipped in their corporeal state (a fitting denouement for the heirs of golden calf worship), the rabbis supply the intelligibility by memorizing previous rabbinical interpretations and embellishments (*qere)* and adding them to the material object that constitutes the text of the scroll (*ketiv).*

The whole process of mutilating the Scriptures and then leaving the decision on their reading and meaning to a pseudo-priest caste of rabbis is perhaps the ultimate symbolic put-down of the Bible.

Here it is necessary to reflect on the fact that Judaism does not in any manner entail the worship of Yahweh, the God of the Bible.

Judaism's god is the Jewish people themselves as embodied in their rabbis. Judaism is worship of Jewish blood in the person of the rabbi. The Jewish "race" itself is rendered god by this means.

The dumbshow surrounding how to read the *sefer Torah* scrolls, illustrates this. In studying the Talmudic discussions concerning this issue, various schools of thought are advanced concerning the superior intelligibility of vowels versus consonants or vice versa. [29]

The arcane mechanics of stresses, pauses, accents, glosses, omissions and versifications are batted back and forth, until an outsider looking at this farrago can only scratch his head in wonder at how any understanding of the text of the scrolls will ever be reached.

And that's exactly the point. What is being taught in these Talmudic passages is not how to find the key to the mutilated Torah texts as presented in the scroll-totems. Understanding the redacted Biblical text is not the goal of the Talmudic lesson being imparted, but rather the lesson centers on the ambiguity of the written Scriptures when

---

[29]Sanhedrin 3b-4b, Megillah 25b.

viewed without the intervention of rabbinic interpretation.

The message Satan has been whispering in the ears of those imbued with the unclean Talmudic/Kabbalistic spirit since this crowd first swarmed the glittering yellow-red statue of a calf and offered it obeisance, is that the written text of the Old Testament is not sufficient. It is incomplete and lacking. Indeed, Judaism teaches that it is utterly incomprehensible and ultimately mute *unless* it is taught out of the mouths of the Talmudic rabbis.

The barely concealed message of the previously cited Talmudic discussions is that it is the rabbis and not the Bible, who are the source of all godly gnosis, wisdom and holiness.

Judaism is the very theology of Biblical nullification, exactly as Christ stated. It has evolved a whole system of Scriptural nullification and rigidly codified it.

The symbol of that nullification is the synagogue's idolatrous Torah scroll, which contains not the Old Testament Scriptures, but a mockery of them. They have been suppressed, expurgated and re-written to such an extent as to be made all but unrecognizable to anyone except the rabbis.

The Talmud elucidates the core horror at the center of this heart of darkness by teaching that the falsification of Scripture is central to understanding the Scriptures; and that this system of falsification was secretly sanctioned by Moses:

"The vocalization of the scribes, the omissions of the scribes and the Scripture words that are read but not written and the Scripture passages that are written but not read, are practices (*hlkh*) revealed to Moses from Sinai."[30]

In other words, rabbinic tradition, claiming the sanction of Moses himself, decides how the Bible texts are read, what parts are suppressed or misrepresented and what words from the oral tradition (*hlkh*) of the elders will be authoritatively promulgated. The presentation and meaning of the Bible text is thereby inextricably chained

---

[30]Nedarim 37a & 38b.

to rabbinic tradition.

Judaism teaches that the key to the meaning of the Bible is not in the Bible itself. It resides exclusively in the secret lore (*hlkh*) of the rabbis.

How different is this epistemology of Judaism from that of Christ, who proclaimed that He said "nothing in secret" (John 18:20).

It is secrecy, priestcraft, occult tradition and the personality cult of the rabbis which alone determines, in Judaism, how the Bible will be manipulated.

Examples of Nullification

The Talmud itself admits that most of its endless rules and regulations, have little Scriptural basis and that the oral tradition of the Mishnah supersedes the written laws of the Scriptures:

"The absolution of vows (*Kol Nidrei*) hovers in the air, for it has nothing in the Torah on which to depend. The laws of the Sabbath, festal offerings, and sacrilege--lo, they are like mountains hanging by a string, for they have little Scripture for many laws." [31]

It is an interesting fact that, what Christ termed heavy burdens these Pharisees bind the people with, are, by their own admission, "hanging by a string," when it comes to Scriptural justification.

The Talmudic "sage" declares unambiguously the basis of the religion of the rabbis:

"Some teachings were handed on orally, and some things were handed on in writing...we conclude that the ones that are handed on orally are more precious."[32]

It is the Mishnah which is believed to contain the revelations of God to Moses at Sinai. Yet, in the introduction to the Yale University English translation of the Mishnah, it is stated that "The Mishnah is a document of imagination and fantasy..."[33]

------

[31]Hagigah, 1:8.

[32]Hagigah 1:7.V.

[33]*The Mishnah: A New Translation* [New Haven,

Since God and Moses were not fantasists, this is a frank admission of the entirely man-made nature of the Mishnah-Talmud:

"(T)he Mishnah...is remarkably indifferent to the Hebrew Scriptures...The Mishnah is made up of the sayings bearing the names of authorities who lived in the late first and second centuries (A.D.)

"In fact, the Mishnah is...a principal holy book of Judaism. The Mishnah has been and is now memorized in the circle of all those who participate in the religion, Judaism...the two great documents formed around the Mishnah and so shaped as to serve, in part, as commentaries upon Mishnah, namely, the Babylonian Talmud and the Palestinian Talmud, form the center of the curriculum of Judaism as a living religion." [34]

The Mishnah is the well-spring of the man-made religion of Judaism, from which spout centuries of interpretations and never-ending additional rabbinical supplements, expansions, and expostulations in a huge compendium of arid Talmudic pedantry and pettifogging -- augmentation and commentaries upon commentaries -- that begins with the supplement to the Mishnah, the Tosefta.

Because it is regarded by the rabbis as the supreme revelation of Sinai, having been passed down orally, in secret, across millennia, the Mishnah is a law unto itself which does not need to claim a Biblical basis for its authority.

"In Splendid Isolation from Scripture"

Rabbi Jacob Neusner states: "On the surface, Scripture plays little role in the Mishnaic system. The Mishnah rarely cites a verse of Scripture, refers to Scripture as an entity, links its own ideas to those of Scripture, or lays claim to originate in what Scripture has said, even by indirect or remote allusion to a Scriptural verse of teaching...Formally, redactionally, and linguistically the Mishnah stands in splendid isolation from Scripture.

CT: Yale University Press, 1988], p. xvii.

[34]Ibid., pp. xiii and xv.

"...the Mishnah constitutes *torah*. It too is a statement of revelation, 'Torah revealed to Moses at Sinai.' But this part of revelation has come down in a form different from the well-known, written part, the Scripture. This tradition truly deserves the name 'tradition,' because for a long time it was handed down orally, not in writing, until given the written formulation now before us in the Mishnah.

"...Since some of the named authorities in the chain of tradition appear throughout the materials of the Mishnah, the claim is that what these people say comes to them from Sinai through the processes of *qabbalah* and *massoret*-- handing down, 'traditioning.' So the reason...that the Mishnah does not cite Scripture is that it does not *have* to." [35]

From this statement of Rabbi Neusner, we deduce that the Mishnah was the autonomous oral tradition that existed in the time of Christ and to which Jesus made direct and accurate reference to as the "tradition of the Elders."

Moreover, Neusner alludes to the *qabbalah* (more commonly spelled Kabbalah), the Jewish book of secret Satanic teachings, as the "process" by which the Mishnah was transmitted. This Kabbalah arose in Babylon, as did the initial texts of the Talmud and both are heavily influenced by the abominable occult practices and superstitions of Babylon.

Judaism as Self-Worship

One manifestation of this superstition is found in Judaism's self-worship. In Judaism the rabbi is the Torah incarnate. He actualizes this divine status through memorization and vain repetition of the Talmud and Talmudic interpretations of the Tanakh (Old Testament), in a manner similar to the import Eastern religions attach to mantric incantations.

The Talmud mantra is believed to give the rabbi supernatural power and his intrinsic superiority and divinity is made manifest by this means. He himself now becomes an object of worship, like the Torah scroll, because,

[35] Ibid, pp. xxxv and xxxvi.

having achieved his full manifestation as the incarnate Torah, he himself becomes the main source of Jewish salvation.

The Talmud has God declare: "If a man occupies himself with the study of Torah, works of charity, and prays with the community, I account it to him as if he had redeemed me and my children from among the nations of the world."[36]

"Those who engage in talmudic study make it possible for themselves, their families, their financial supporters and, to some extent, other Jews to enter paradise." [37]

This is the empty "salvation" offered by the religion of Judaism in the wake of the rejection and crucifixion of the Messiah and the destruction of the Temple, which the Messiah prophesied.

Having rejected their Messiah, the Pharisees became more corrupt than ever and out of this corruption came the fully institutionalized nullification of the Old Testament, and its replacement by self-worship.

The totemic, pagan-Babylonian root of this process of self-idolatry, is hinted at by the fact of the rabbi's object-orientation, rather than his spiritual orientation.

It is not the rabbi's understanding and grasp of the Torah that makes him a veritable incarnate god and object of worship,[38] but rather his rote memorization and repetition of the material object, i.e. the texts themselves, because:

"...the Babylonian Talmud represents God in the flesh..."[39]

Hence, the authority of the Mishnah is derived from the authority of the rabbi, because whatever the rabbi declares to be from Sinai is from Sinai, because the rabbi is Sinai

---

[36]Berakhot 8A.

[37]Shahak and Mezvinsky, [op. cit.] p. 27.

[38]Ibid. The authors refer explicitly to the "worship" of "charismatic rabbis" (p. 26).

[39] Neusner, *Rabbinic Judaism*, op. cit., p. 62.

incarnate. [40]

Since the Mishnah stands alone as an authority, without justification Biblically, it fell to the later rabbinical writings of the Talmud, such as the *Sifra*, which do comment at length upon Scripture, to attempt to correlate Mishnaic teachings with those of the Torah.[41]

In considering all of this, we may call to mind the situation of the Christian ecclesia today, which is occupied by those who are so completely smitten, from the pope and the ministers of the major Protestant denominations, on down to the lowliest street-corner, fundamentalist preacher, with the presumed divine racial prestige, Biblical knowledge and Old Testament wisdom of the rabbis of Judaism.

Cast off to the sidelines are those evangelical Christians who refuse any doctrine or authority that contradicts the Bible (*sola Scriptura*), and are castigated as "extremists" and "haters" by their erstwhile pastors. Their attendance at almost any modern church is a source of scandal and embarrassment to the churchmen. This Christian remnant exists largely in house-churches and other small gatherings sprinkled across the countryside.

By the same token, protesting Catholics see in the pronouncements and symbolic actions of the popes since John XXIII and particularly in the pontificate of John Paul II, a radical departure from nearly 2,000 years of Christian teaching and practice.

In March, 2000, John Paul II turned his coat in *verbo* and *facto,* making obeisance in Jerusalem to the religious heirs of the Pharisees who ordered Jesus' execution. The Pope apologized to them for "displays of anti-semitism directed against the Jews by Christians at any time in

---

[40]This circular reasoning is a fixture of many controversies, where opposition is silenced by Jewish insistence on their own certainty and authority, after which the case is closed and to proceed further would entail "anti-semitism."

[41]References to the Torah in Judaism are invariably misleading. By dictionary definition, Torah denotes the books of the Old Testament (Tanakh). But in Judaism, the word Torah can signify the Talmud alone or both the Talmud and the Tanakh.

any place." [42]

This apology would seem to encompass the deeds of thousands of saints and luminaries of the Church from John Chrysostom onward to most of the literary canon of the West, including Dante's *Paradisio,* which hails the Roman destruction of the Temple as "living justice," and Chaucer 's "The Prioress' Tale."

The disapprobatory shadow presumably also falls on Rome's own canonized Pope Pius X who, when asked in 1904 to recognize Palestine as the rightful Jewish homeland, told Zionist Theodore Herzl, "As the head of the Church, I cannot answer you otherwise: the Jews have not recognized the Lord; therefore we cannot recognize the Jewish people." [43]

Christianity has, to a large extent, been taken over by the religion of Judaism and become a fossil more properly distinguished as Judeo-Churchianity. It is interesting to compare the situation in our churches with a passage from the Talmud:

"There was a certain gentile who came before Rabbi Shammai. The gentile said to him, 'How many Torahs do you have?'

"The rabbi replied, 'Two, one in writing, one memorized.'

"The gentile then said to him, 'As to the one in writing, I believe you. As to the memorized one, I do not believe you. Convert me on condition that you will teach me only the Torah that is in writing.'

"The rabbi rebuked the gentile and threw him out."[44]

The Gentile in the preceding Talmud citation trusted only the Bible and was expelled by the rabbi because he refused the teaching which was based on the oral traditions

---

[42]*Jewish Chronicle*, March 31, 2000.

[43]Sergio I. Minerbi, *The Vatican & Zionism* [NY: Oxford Univ. Press, 1990], p. 100. Also implicitly consigned to the hall of shame by John Paul II is Benedict XIV, who warned that Jewish officials in Poland were using Christian peasants as virtual slaves; cf. *A Quo Primum,* June 14, 1751.

[44]Shabbat 31a; Rabbi Nathan XV:V.1.

of the elders. In precisely the same manner, true Christians today are cast out of their churches because they are faithful to the Gospel and reject the influence of and the respect paid to Judaism, the religion which is based upon the traditions of the elders and the creation of loopholes in God's law.

"But though we or an angel from heaven, preach any other Gospel unto you than that which we have preached unto you, let him be accursed...For do I now persuade men or God? Or do I seek to please men? For if I yet pleased men, I should not be the servant of Christ." (Galatians 1:8-10).

As for the loopholes, Shmuel Safrai points out that in the Talmud's Gittin Tractate, the Talmud nullifies the Biblical teaching concerning money-lending:

"Hillel decreed the *prozbul* for the betterment of the world. The *prozbul* is a legal fiction which allows debts to be collected after the Sabbatical year and it was Hillel's intention thereby to overcome the fear that money-lenders had of losing their money."[45]

There is also the Talmudic nullification of the sin of David: as a humbling motif of imperfection even in the elect, and of sin and redemption, Christians have long pondered the sobering lesson entailed within the Biblical account of King David's adultery with Bathsheba.

But the religion of Judaism will have none of this. According to the Babylonian Talmud, "whoever says King David sinned is mistaken." The Talmud states that the practice in those days was for men going to war to give their wives conditional divorces. Bathsheba was no longer married and hence the Talmud decrees that David did not sin. [46]

What the Talmudic rabbis are actually saying is that it is God who is mistaken, because the Word of God clearly declares that David sinned by killing Uriah the Hittite *and* taking his wife: "Now therefore the sword shall never

---

[45] *The Literature of the Sages,* Part One, p. 164.

[46] Richard Horowitz, *N.Y. Times,* Jan. 2, 1995.

depart from thine house because thou hast despised me and hast taken the wife of Urriah the Hittite to be thy wife." (II Samuel 12:10).

So who are we to believe, the word of God as found in the Old Testament book of Samuel, or the word of the Pharisees as found in the Babylonian Talmud?

Followers of the religion of Judaism believe the Talmud. Followers of Christ understand just what such Talmudic falsification of the Word of God entails: "Woe unto you, scribes and Pharisees, hypocrites! For ye shut up the kingdom of heaven against men. For ye neither enter in yourselves; neither do ye let others enter." (Matthew 23:13).

In Baba Kama 83b-84a, Talmudic logic intricately weaves and falsifies portions of the Books of Numbers and Leviticus, ripping them out of their context to demonstrate that the oft-cited passage from Exodus 21:24 ("An eye for an eye and a tooth for a tooth"), does not actually denote the obvious, literal meaning, but is really a command to make monetary restitution.

The Talmud (with the Kabbalah) is Judaism's holiest book. The supremacy of the Talmud over the Bible in the Israeli state may also be seen in the case of the black Ethiopian Falasha. Ethiopians are knowledgeable of the Old Testament. However, their religion is so ancient it pre-dates the Scribes' Talmud, of which the Ethiopians have no knowledge.

"The problem is that Ethiopian Jewish tradition goes no further than the Bible or Torah; the later Talmud and other commentaries that form the basis of modern traditions never came their way." [47]

Because they are not traffickers in Talmudic tradition, the black Ethiopians are discriminated against and have been forbidden by the Israelis to perform marriages, funerals and other services in the Israeli state.

Rabbi Joseph D. Soloveitchik is regarded as one of the most influential rabbis of the 20th century, the "unchallenged leader" of Orthodox Judaism and the top international authority on halakhah (Jewish religious law).

---

[47]N.Y. Times, Sept. 29, 1992, p.4.

Soloveitchik was responsible for instructing and ordaining more than 2,000 rabbis, "an entire generation" of Jewish leadership.

N.Y. Times religion reporter Ari Goldman described the basis of the rabbi's authority: "Soloveitchik came from a long line of distinguished Talmudic scholars...Until his early 20s, he devoted himself almost exclusively to the study of the Talmud...He came to Yeshiva University's Elchanan Theological Seminary where he remained the pre-eminent teacher in the Talmud...He held the title of Leib Merkin professor of Talmud...sitting with his feet crossed in front of a table bearing an open volume of the Talmud." [48]

Nowhere does Goldman refer to Soloveitchik's knowledge of the Bible as the basis for being one of the leading authorities on Jewish law.

The rabbi's credentials are all predicated upon his mastery of the Talmud. Other studies are clearly secondary. Britain's *Jewish Chronicle* of March 26, 1993 states that in religious school (yeshiva), Jewish students are "devoted to the Talmud to the exclusion of everything else."

Jewish scholar Hyam Maccoby, in *Judaism on Trial*, quotes Rabbi Yehiel ben Joseph: "Further, without the Talmud, we would not be able to understand passages in the Bible...God has handed this authority to the sages and tradition is a necessity as well as scripture. The Sages also made enactments of their own...anyone who does not study the Talmud cannot understand Scripture."

There are two versions of the Talmud, the Jerusalem Talmud and the Babylonian Talmud.

The Babylonian Talmud is regarded as the authoritative version: "The authority of the Babylonian Talmud is also greater than that of the Jerusalem Talmud. In cases of doubt the former is decisive." [49]

The Talmud passages reprinted in the following pages

---

[48] N.Y. Times, April 10, 1993, p. 38.

[49] R.C. Musaph-Andriesse, *From Torah to Kabbalah: A Basic Introduction to the Writings of Judaism*, p. 40.

come from the Jewish-authorized Babylonian Talmud. Look them up for yourself. [50]

This documentation is published in the hope of liberating all people, *including Jewish people,* from the corrosive malice and racist loathing of this Talmudic hate literature, which is the paramount manual for adherents of Judaism the world over.

The implementation by Jewish supremacists of Talmudic anti-Gentile law and jurisprudence has caused untold suffering throughout history and in Lebanon and occupied Palestine, is used as a justification for the mass murder of Arab civilians.[51] The Talmud specifically defines all who are not Jews as non-human animals.

Hitting a Jew is the same as hitting God
Sanhedrin 58b. If a gentile hits a Jew, the gentile must be killed.

O.K. to Cheat Non-Jews
Sanhedrin 57a. A Jew need not pay a gentile the wages owed him for work.

Jews Have Superior Legal Status
Baba Kamma 37b. "If an ox of an Israelite gores an ox of a Canaanite there is no liability; but if an ox of a Canaanite gores an ox of an Israelite...the payment is to be in full."

Jews May Steal from Non-Jews
Baba Mezia 24a. If a Jew finds an object lost by a gentile it does not have to be returned. (Affirmed also in Baba Kamma 113b). Sanhedrin 76a. God will not spare a Jew who "marries his daughter to an old man or takes a wife for his infant son or returns a lost article to a gentile..."

Jews May Rob and Kill Non-Jews
Sanhedrin 57a. When a Jew murders a gentile there will be no death penalty. What a Jew steals from a gentile he may keep.

---

[50]The material in this section was researched by Alan R. Critchley and Michael A. Hoffman II.

[51]Shahak and Mezvinsky (op. cit.), furnish exhaustive evidence of this in their book-length thesis.

Baba Kamma 37b. The gentiles are outside the protection of the law and God has "exposed their money to Israel."

"Relying upon the Code of Maimonides and the Halacha, the Gush Emunim leader Rabbi Israel Ariel stated: 'A Jew who killed a non-Jew is exempt from human judgment and has not violated the religious prohibition of murder.'"[52]

Jews May Lie to Non-Jews

Baba Kamma 113a. Jews may use lies ("subterfuges") to circumvent a Gentile.

Non-Jewish Children are Sub-Human

Yebamoth 98a. All gentile children are animals.

Abodah Zarah 36b. Gentile girls are in a state of niddah (filth) from birth.

Insults Against Blessed Mary

Sanhedrin 106a. Says Jesus' mother was a whore: "She who was the descendant of princes and governors played the harlot with carpenters." Also in footnote #2 to Shabbath 104b of the Soncino edition, it is stated that in the "uncensored" text of the Talmud it is written that Jesus mother, "Miriam the hairdresser," had sex with many men.

Jesus in the Talmud

It is the standard disinformation practice of apologists for the Talmud to deny that it contains any scurrilous references to Jesus. According to this charade, to assert the truth that the Talmud contains disgusting and pornographic blasphemies against Jesus is "hateful and anti-semitic."

The truth cannot be hateful however, except in the eyes of those who hate the truth. Truth cannot be "anti" anyone, for the truth sets everyone free.

While major Jewish organizations charged with the mission of deceiving Christians and Gentiles through their mouthpiece media, such as the ADL and the Simon Wiesenthal Center, continue to stonewall and maintain the covert charade by denying that there is anything in the Talmud which libels the Christian savior, the position of certain Jewish scholars over the years has undergone a change and more have leaned toward revealing the actual

---

[52]Ibid., p. 71.

contents of the Talmud on this subject.

In the latter part of the 20th century, for example, Hyam Maccoby was willing to concede in a book intended mainly for scholars and specialists, that it "seems" that:

"The Talmud contains a few explicit references to Jesus...These references are certainly not complimentary...There seems little doubt that the account of the execution of Jesus on the eve of Passover does refer to the Christian Jesus...The passage in which Jesus' punishment in hell is described also seems to refer to the Christian Jesus. It is a piece of anti-Christian polemic dating from the post-70 CE period..." [53]

Maccoby's qualification that the Talmud "seems" to attack Jesus Christ, was gradually replaced by more unambiguous confirmation by other Jewish scholars later in the 20th century. But whether or not Jewish sources confirm, qualify or deny it, we have documentary evidence of the disgusting and hateful references to Jesus *in the Talmudic texts themselves*, in Sanhedrin 43a, Sanhedrin 107b, Sotah 47a, Shabbos 104b and Gittin 57a.

In 1984 Prof. Robert Goldenberg wrote:

"Many famous legends about personalities in the Bible make their first appearance in the Talmud...rabbinic narrative includes folklore, stories about angels and demons, and gossip about all sorts of surprising people (Nero became a convert to Judaism, Jesus was an Egyptian magician and so on)." [54]

By 1999, certain Orthodox Jewish organizations were even more forthcoming, openly admitting that the Talmud describes Jesus as a sorcerer and a demented sex freak. These Jewish organizations make this admission perhaps out of the conceit that Jewish supremacy is so well-entrenched in the modern world that they need not concern themselves with adverse reactions.

On the website of the Orthodox Jewish, Chabad-

---

[53] Hyam Maccoby, *Judaism on Trial*, pp. 26-27.

[54] Robert Goldenberg, "Talmud," *Back to the Sources: Reading the Classic Jewish Texts*, (op. cit.), p. 170.

Lubavitch group--one of the largest and most powerful Jewish organizations in the world--we find the following statement, accompanied by citations from the Talmud:

"The Talmud (Babylonian edition) records other sins of 'Jesus the Nazarene.' 1. 'He and his disciples practiced sorcery and black magic, led Jews astray into idolatry, and were sponsored by foreign, gentile powers for the purpose of subverting Jewish worship (Sanhedrin 43a).

2. "He was sexually immoral, worshipped statues of stone (a brick is mentioned), was cut off from the Jewish people for his wickedness, and refused to repent (Sanhedrin 107b; Sotah 47a).

3. "He learned witchcraft in Egypt...(Shabbos 104b)." [55]

(End quote from Chabad-Lubavitch).

Gittin 57a says Jesus is in hell, being boiled in "hot excrement."

Sanhedrin 43a says Jesus was executed because he practiced sorcery: "It is taught that on the eve of Passover Jesus was hung, and forty days before this the proclamation was made: Jesus is to be stoned to death because he has practiced sorcery and has lured the people to idolatry...He was an enticer and of such thou shalt not pity or condone."

Rabbi Lies to Induce Mary to Tell the Truth About How Jesus Was Conceived

"The elders were once sitting in the gate when two young lads passed by; one covered his head and the other uncovered his head. Of him who uncovered his head Rabbi Eliezer remarked that he is a bastard. Rabbi Joshua remarked that he is the son of a niddah (a child conceived during a woman's menstrual period). Rabbi Akiba said that he is both a bastard and a son of a niddah.

"They said, 'What induced you to contradict the opinion of your colleagues?' He replied, "I will prove it concerning him." He went to the lad's mother and found her sitting in the market selling beans.

"He said to her, 'My daughter, if you will answer the question I

[55]Quoted from the Chabad-Lubavitch, "Noah's Covenant Website,"at http://www.noahide.com/yeshu.htm on June 20, 2000; a printed copy of which is preserved in our files.

will put to you, I will bring you to the world to come' (eternal life). She said to him, 'Swear it to me.'

"Rabbi Akiba, *taking the oath with his lips but annulling it in his heart,* said to her, 'What is the status of your son?' She replied, 'When I entered the bridal chamber I was niddah (menstruating) and my husband kept away from me; but my best man had intercourse with me and this son was born to me.' Consequently the child was both a bastard and the son of a niddah.

"It was declared, '..Blessed be the God of Israel Who Revealed His Secret to Rabbi Akiba..." (Kallah 51a, emphasis supplied).

In addition to the theme that God rewards clever liars, the preceding Talmud passage is actually about Jesus Christ (the bastard boy who "uncovered his head" and was conceived in the filth of menstruation). The boy's adulterous mother in this Talmud story is the mother of Christ, Blessed Mary (called Miriam and sometimes, Miriam the hairdresser, in the Talmud).

Dr. Israel Shahak of Jerusalem's Hebrew University states:

"The Editio Princeps of the complete Code of Talmudic Law, Maimonides' *Mishneh Torah* -- replete not only with the most offensive precepts against all Gentiles but also with explicit attacks on Christianity and on Jesus (after whose name the author adds piously, 'May the name of the wicked perish')... [56]

"According to the Talmud, Jesus was executed by a proper rabbinical court for idolatry, inciting other Jews to idolatry, and contempt of rabbinical authority. All classical Jewish sources which mention his execution are quite happy to take responsibility for it; in the talmudic account the Romans are not even mentioned.

"The more popular accounts--which were nevertheless taken quite seriously--such as the notorious Toldot Yeshu are even worse, for in addition to the above crimes they accuse him of witchcraft. The very name 'Jesus' was for Jews a symbol of all that is abominable and this popular tradition still persists...

"The Hebrew form of the name Jesus--Yeshu--was interpreted as an acronym for the curse, 'may his name and memory be wiped

[56]Israel Shahak, *Jewish History, Jewish Religion,* (London: Pluto Press, 1994) p. 21.

out,' which is used as an extreme form of abuse. In fact, anti-zionist Orthodox Jews (such as Neturey Qarta) sometimes refer to Herzl as 'Herzl Jesus' and I have found in religious zionist writings expressions such as "Nasser Jesus" and more recently 'Arafat Jesus."[57]

The historian and linguist Daniel-Rops writes:

"We certainly cannot look to the Talmuds for any direct historical information regarding Jesus. All that the rabbis let us know about him is hostile, insulting and malevolent. Sometimes he is referred to under the name of Balaam the son of Behor, 'the false prophet' who led Israel astray; sometimes under his real name of Jesus of Nazareth, but always with some insulting qualification, such as the liar, the impostor or the bastard.

"These fables even crystallized in the rabbinical tradition to form a blasphemous pseudo-biography, the *Toledoth Jeshua* which circulated among the Jews...According to this compilation, Jesus was the illegitimate son of Mary, the wife of a perfumer and of a Roman soldier, called Pandara or Panthera. He was taken by his stepfather to Egypt where he studied sorcery and was thus enabled to seduce Israel. He was arrested as an agitator and a sorcerer and turned over to the Sanhedrin, spending forty days in the pillory before he was stoned and hanged at the Feast of the Passover.

"This repellant fable is so full of absurdities that it is idle to combat it; the stepfather of Jesus is called Josue ben Parania, although the personage of that name died 78 years before the Christian era. The reference to Mary as a perfumer comes obviously from confusion

---

[57]Israel Shahak, *Jewish History, Jewish Religion*, (op. cit.) pp. 97-98, 118. It's interesting to note that while the sacred texts of Judaism gloat over the death of Christ and "are happy to take responsibility for it," the official position of the Jewish Anti-Defamation League (ADL), as imposed on the producers of the Oberammergau Passion Play (*Detroit Free Press*, Feb. 17, 1990) is that the Romans alone, not the Pharisees, were guilty of Christ's death and that it was Pilate, not Caiphas, who actively conspired in His assassination. This line has been endorsed by the National Conference of Catholic Bishops (ADL press release, April 27, 2000) and by the pope, who conferred the Knighthood of St. Gregory on ADL officer Leonard Zakim (*Boston Globe*, Nov. 4, 1999). It is also showcased in Hollywood films such as the CBS-TV "miniseries" *Jesus*, (broadcast May, 2000).

with Mary Magdalen because 'Magdala' can mean a hairdresser, while the name Panthera is probably due to an imperfect understanding of Greek since *parthenos* means virgin and the Christians have always referred to Christ as the Son of the Virgin." [58]

Talmud Attacks Christians
and Christian Books

Rosh Hashanah 17a. Christians (*minim*[59]) and others who reject the Talmud will go to hell and be punished there for all generations.

Sanhedrin 90a. Those who read the New Testament ("uncanonical books") will have no portion in the world to come.

Shabbat 116a. Jews must destroy the books of the Christians, i.e. the New Testament: "The books of the minim may not be saved from a fire, but they must be burnt."

Prof. Shahak reports that the Israelis burned hundreds of New Testament Bibles in occupied Palestine on March 23, 1980. [60]

Sick and Insane Teachings of the Talmud

Yebamoth 63a. Declares that agriculture is the lowest of occupations.

Gittin 69a. To heal his flesh a Jew should take dust that lies within the shadow of an outdoor toilet, mix with honey and eat it.

Shabbath 41a. The law regulating the rule for how to urinate in a holy way is given.

Abodah Zarah 22a-22b. Gentiles prefer sex with cows.

Yebamoth 63a. States that Adam had sexual intercourse with all the animals in the Garden of Eden.

Abodah Zarah 17a. States that there is not a whore in

---

[58]Daniel-Rops, *Jesus and His Times,* [op. cit.], pp. 66-67.

[59]The 12th invocation of the *Amidah* (the central prayer of Judaism recited three times daily) is the *birkat ha-minim*, the curse on Christians. Cf. *Lingua Franca,* Nov. 1999, p. 5.

[60] Shahak, op. cit., p. 21.

the world that the Talmudic sage Rabbi Eleazar has not had sex with.

Hagigah 27a. Declares that no rabbi can ever go to hell.

Yebamoth 59b. A woman who had intercourse with a beast is eligible to marry a Jewish priest. A woman who has sex with a demon is also eligible to marry a Jewish priest.

Erubin 21b. Whosoever disobeys the rabbis deserves death and will be punished by being boiled in hot excrement in hell.

Baba Mezia 59b. A sly rabbi debates God and through trickery defeats Him. God admits the rabbi won the debate.

Moed Kattan 17a. If a Jew is tempted to do evil he should go to a city where he is not known and do the evil there.

Gittin 70a. The Rabbis taught: "On coming from a privy (outdoor toilet) a man should not have sexual intercourse until he has waited long enough to walk half a mile, because the demon of the privy is with him for that time; if he does, his children will be epileptic."

Gittin 69b. To heal the disease of pleurisy ("catarrh") a Jew should "take the excrement of a white dog and knead it with balsam, but if he can possibly avoid it he should not eat the dog's excrement as it loosens the limbs."

Pesahim 111a. It is forbidden for dogs, women or palm trees to pass between two men, nor may others walk between dogs, women or palm trees. Special dangers are involved if the women are menstruating or sitting at a crossroads.

Pesahim 111a: "If two women sit at a crossroads, one on this side and the other on the other side, and they face one another, they are certainly witches."

Menahoth 43b-44a. A Jewish man is obligated to say the following prayer every day: "Thank you God for not making me a gentile, a woman or a slave."

Sexual Intercourse
with Little Girls is Permissible

Ketubot 11b: "If a grown-up man has intercourse with a little girl, it is nothing, for having intercourse with a girl less than three years old is like putting a finger in the eye."

Though the Talmud's permission for the heinous crime of child molestation is virtually unknown among the public and is never mentioned in the establishment media, among Talmud researchers it is notorious.

This portion of tractate Ketubot concerns Halakhic definitions of sexual intercourse. In this particular ruling it is stated that copulation with girls below the age of three cannot be considered sexual activity because, although penetration ruptures her hymen, such intercourse is merely "like putting a finger in the eye," since the hymen at this age will eventually regenerate (just as a finger stuck in an eye will cause the eye to water, yet the eye will heal and return to its former state, so the hymen of a girl under three will rupture during intercourse but will heal later).

Once her hymen grows back, the little girl is regarded as lawfully still a virgin. Hence the Talmud recognizes no sexual intercourse as having occurred and therefore exacts no penalty for coitus with a female child of less than three years of age.

The Talmud's Tall Tales of a Roman Holocaust

There are two early "Holocaust" tales from the Talmud. Gittin 57b claims that four billion Jews were killed by the Romans in the city of Bethar. Gittin 58a claims that 16 million Jewish children were wrapped in scrolls and burned alive by the Romans. (Ancient demography indicates that there were not 16 million Jews in the entire world at that time, much less 16 million Jewish children or four billion Jews).

A Revealing Admission

Abodah Zarah 70a. The question was asked of the rabbi whether wine stolen in Pumbeditha might be used or if it was defiled, due to the fact that the thieves might have been Gentiles (a Gentile touching wine would make the wine unclean). The rabbi says not to worry, that the wine is permissible for Jewish use because the majority of the thieves in Pumbeditha, the place where the wine was stolen, are Jews. (Also cf. Rosh Hashanah 25b). [61]

Even the Best of Women are Witches

Kiddushin 66c: "The best of the gentiles -- kill him; the best of snakes -- smash its skull; the best of women -- is filled with witchcraft." [62]

Mishnah Abot 2:7: "The more possessions the more worry; the more wives, the more witchcraft" (Hillel, first century A.D.)

Rabbah 45:5 libels Sarah, the wife of Abraham, saying she used witchcraft (specifically, the "evil eye") to cause Hagar to have a miscarriage. This Talmudic account of Sarah follows the *modus operandi* of the Talmudic witch, Johani, the daughter of Retibi, who also used the evil eye to cause spontaneous abortion. [63]

Examples of punishment of Jewish witches in the Talmud are almost non-existent, while in at least one case, Gentiles accused of witchcraft were hanged en masse by a rabbi. [64] Johani the Jewish witch is never punished, perhaps because

---

[61] Dr. Israel Shahak and his co-author, Prof. Mezvinsky, qualify this injunction thus: "The Halacha permits Jews to rob non-Jews in those locales wherein Jews are stronger than non-Jews. The Halacha prohibits Jews from robbing non-Jews in those locales wherein the non-Jews are stronger." (*Jewish Fundamentalism in Israel*, op. cit., p. 71).

[62] The uncensored version of this text appears in Tractate Soferim, (New York, M. Higer, 1937), 15:7, p. 282. Other versions delete the misogynist slur, cf. Y.N. Epstein & E.Z. Melamed, *Mekhilta d' Rabbi Shimon bar Yohai* [Jerusalem, 1979], p. 51.

[63] B.M. Levin, *Otzar HaGeonim* ("The Treasury of the Geonim"), 11, Sotah [Jerusalem, 1942], pp. 241-242. Also cf. S. Abramson, "Le R. Barukh ben Melekh," Tarbiz 19 (1948), 42-44.

[64] According to Hagigah 77d, Rabbi Simeon ben Shetah hanged 80 women in Ashkelon who were accused of witchcraft, but they were Gentile women, not Jewish.

she is not doing anything contrary to Kabbalistic teaching.[65]

Sanhedrin 25d comments on the Talmudic observation that most Jewish women are witches by observing that "such is the way of the world." By Talmudic standards, Jewish witchcraft is not something extraordinary, it is an inherent quality of Jewish women, along with other problems endemic to this "sack of excrement" (Shabbat 152b) and "valueless treasure" (Sanhedrin 100b), including a proclivity for murder (Peskita Rabbati, 107b). These female attributes ascribed by the Talmud are regarded as ineradicable and a foreshadowing of qualities that will predominate once the "*tikkun olam*" is implemented.

Moreover, witchcraft in the Talmud is not just an attribute of Jewish women. The Jewish books of black magic of the Babylonian era, *Sefer HaRazim* and *Harba de Mosheh,* were both compiled by Jewish males, and Sanhedrin 17a decrees that to be qualified for appointment to the Sanhedrin (religious court), a man must be a practitioner of sorcery.

Many revered rabbis used magic and witchcraft to prevail over their enemies or to demonstrate their thaumaturgic powers. Rabbi Simon ben Yohai used magic to turn an opponent into a "heap of bones" (Shevi'it 38d). Other rabbis used sorcery to create a calf (Sanhedrin 65b).

Pharisaic Rituals

Erubin 21b. "Rabbi Akiba said to him, "Give me some water to wash my hands."

"It will not suffice for drinking," the other complained, "will it suffice for washing your hands?"

"What can I do?' the former replied, "when for neglecting the words of the Rabbis one deserves death? It is better

---

[65]*Tikkun olam* is the name for the Kabbalistic "redemption of the world," but the Jewish concept of redemption is very different from what that term signifies to the goyim. A deeper understanding can be gleaned from the teachings of one of the major Kabbalistic "sages," Rabbi Isaac Luria, who said that after *tikkun* was accomplished the spirit of Cain would prevail on earth. Cf. Gershom Scholem, *Kabbalah* [Jerusalem: Keter Publishing House 1974; reprinted 1978 by the New American Library, New York], p. 163.

that I myself should die than that I transgress against the opinion of my colleagues." (This is the oral tradition's ritual hand washing condemned by Jesus in Matthew 15: 1-9 as "commandments of men" falsely represented as doctrine).

Genocide Advocated by the Talmud

Soferim 15, Rule 10. This is the saying of Rabbi Simon ben Yohai: *Tob shebe goyyim harog* ("Even the best of the gentiles should all be killed"). [66]

This Talmud passage has been concealed in some translations.

The *Jewish Encyclopedia* states, "...in the various versions the reading has been altered, 'The best among the Egyptians' being generally substituted." In the Soncino version: "the best of the heathens" (Minor Tractates, Soferim 41a-b). [67]

Yohai's genocide injunction permeates Judaism. Israelis annually take part in a national pilgrimage to the grave of Rabbi Yohai, to honor the rabbi who advocated the extermination of non-Jews.

The obsession with the corpse of Rabbi Simon ben Yohai is at the center of the pilgrimage, which occurs in the spring, coinciding with *Lag b'Omer*, which commemorates the Bar Kochba revolt against the Romans, circa 132-135 A.D., after which, the seeming perennial canon of Jewish "Holocaust lore has it that "a terrible massacre of over *one-half million* Jews" followed.[68]

At Rabbi Yohai's purported grave, tens of thousands of both Khazar and Sephardic Israelis gather to receive

---

[66]This passage is from the original Hebrew of the Babylonian Talmud as quoted by the 1907 *Jewish Encyclopedia,* published by Funk and Wagnalls and compiled by Isidore Singer, under the entry, "Gentile," (p. 617).

[67]*Jewish Press,* June 9, 1989, p. 56B.

[68]Abraham Z. Idelsohn, *The Ceremonies of Judaism* (Cincinnati: National Federation of Temple Brotherhoods, 1930), p. 46. Thanks to Rev. Fr. Christopher Hunter for the loan of this book from his private collection.

"emanations" from his corpse. [69]

On Purim, Feb. 25, 1994, a Brooklyn-born physician and Israeli Army officer, Baruch Goldstein, slaughtered 40 Palestinian civilians, including children, while they knelt in prayer in a mosque in Hebron. 25 Palestinians who protested the massacre were shot to death by Israeli troops under the command of Ehud Barak.

Goldstein was a disciple of the late Brooklyn Rabbi Meir Kahane, who told Mike Wallace of CBS News that his teaching that Arabs are "dogs" is derived "from the Talmud."[70]

There was little that was exceptional about Goldstein's massacre other than the high death toll. In May, 1990, Ami Popper, an Israeli, murdered seven unarmed Palestinian day-laborers at Rishon leZion. Eleven Palestinian civilians who protested the massacre were subsequently shot to death by the Israeli army. [71]

A year before Popper's massacre, Rabbi Moshe Levenger was sentenced to a mere five months in prison for the unprovoked murder of an unarmed Palestinian shopkeeper. Before entering prison, Rabbi Levenger was feted at a party in his honor attended by Israeli President Chaim Herzog and Israeli Army Gen. Yitzhak Mordechai. Rabbi Moshe Neriya published a statement for the occasion,

[69]Similar obsessions may be observed amid the Bratslavers who have no living Grand Rabbi, believing instead that they receive emanations from the corpse of Rabbi Nachman of Bratslav (1772-1810), the great-grandson of the Baal Shem Tov. Rabbi Nachman ordered his followers to his grave in Ukraine every Rosh Hashanah in perpetuity, and thousands have dutifully made this pilgrimage to his *Kayver Tzaddikim* every year since the Napoleonic era. Two Kabbalist rabbis of considerable stature, Moses Cordovero and Solomon Alkabez note the magical significance of Jewish cadavers in their book, *Tomer Devorah,* portraying them as a kind of cosmic battery by which God revitalizes Himself.

[70]CBS *60 Minutes*, "Kahane."

[71]*L.A. Times*, May 23, 1990, p. A4.

enjoining Jews to "shoot Arabs left and right without thinking and without hesitating."[72]

University of Jerusalem Prof. Ehud Sprinzak described the philosophy of Israelis like Popper, Levenger, Kahane and Goldstein: "They believe it's God's will that they commit violence against goyim, a Hebrew term for non-Jews." [73]

As a physician, Baruch Goldstein refused to treat Gentiles. He is reported to have said, "I am not willing to treat any non-Jew. I recognize as legitimate only two authorities: Maimonides and Kahane."[74] Goldstein had been the recipient of a certificate of appreciation from the Israeli army medical commander in Hebron. [75]

Goldstein was subsequently disarmed and beaten to death by Arab survivors of his massacre. The Israeli government authorized the closing of some of the busiest Israeli streets in honor of Goldstein's funeral cortege, and the Israeli army provided a guard of honor for Goldstein's tomb. [76]

Israeli journalist Teddy Preuss wrote that Goldstein's "recorded statements and those of his comrades, however, prove that they were willing to exterminate at least two million Palestinians at an opportune moment...As their statements abundantly testify, they see the Arabs as nothing more than disease-spreading rats, lice or other

---

[72]*Wall Street Journal,* May 24, 1990.

[73] *NY Daily News*, Feb. 26, 1994, p. 5.

[74]*Yediot Ahronot,* March 1, 1994. Goldstein was educated in NY at the Yeshiva (Talmud school) of Flatbush; Yeshiva University and Albert Einstein Medical College.

[75]Rabbi Yitzhak Ginsburg, Rabbi Ido Elba, et al., *Baruch Hagever* ("Baruch the Blessed"), [Hebron: Kach, 1995]. A photo of the certificate being conveyed to Goldstein is reproduced on the front cover of the first edition of this large (533 pp.) anthology, published in honor of Goldstein and his massacre. In Rabbi Elba's 26 pp. essay in the book he declares, "...it is a *mitzvah* (divine good deed) to kill every gentile from the nation that is fighting the Jew, even women and children."

[76]*Yediot Ahronot,* Feb. 28, 1994.

loathsome creatures..." [77]

At his funeral, this Jewish mass murderer was eulogized by a host of rabbis, including Dov Lior, who has called for using Arab prisoners in medical experiments.[78] These rabbis not only lauded Goldstein and vociferously cheered his massacre, but advocated further slaughters of Palestinians. These eulogies included Rabbi Israel Ariel's statement that, "The holy martyr Baruch Goldstein is from now on our intercessor in heaven"[79] and Rabbi Yaacov Perrin's declaration that, "One million Arabs are not worth a Jewish fingernail." [80]

"Goldstein is indeed being worshipped as a saint...His intercession before God is asked by (Jewish) pilgrims and it is reported that he cures the ill." [81]

A 1994 poll determined that "at least half of all Israeli Jews would approve of the (Goldstein) massacre, provided that it was not referred to as a massacre..."[82] According to Israeli reporter Gabby Baron, Jewish schoolchildren were "enthused" by Goldstein's massacre. [83]

Baruch Goldstein represents the principles of the Talmud in action. The celebration of Goldstein and his 1994 mass

---

[77]*Davar,* March 4, 1994.

[78]Chaim Bermant, *Jewish Chronicle,* March 4, 1994.

[79]*Yediot Ahronot,* Feb. 28, 1994.

[80]*NY Times,* Feb. 28, 1994, p. 1. Rehavam Ze'evi was somewhat more charitable than Perrin. In 1989 he told the Knesset (Israeli parliament), "Every Jew is worth a thousand Arabs." His statement was videotaped by Visnews and witnessed by MK Yossi Sarid. Cf. *Al-Fajr,* Nov. 6, 1989, p. 15. In a 1983 Knesset session, Israeli Army Chief of Staff Rafael Eitan referred to Palestinians as "cockroaches in a bottle." Cf. *NY Times,* March 6, 1994, p. E16.

[81]*Washington Report on Middle East Affairs,* Jan.-Feb., 1997, p. 102.

[82]Yuval Katz, *Yerushalaim,* March 4, 1994.

[83]*Yediot Ahronot,* March 16, 1994.

murder is based on the Jewish conviction that they have the Talmudic right and halakhic duty to kill Gentiles. Moshe Belogorodsky, an Israeli municipal council member, stated: "It says in the Talmud that when a non-Jew strikes a Jew it's as if he's striking the Divine Presence itself.[84] It's a desecration of God's name. What Baruch (Goldstein) did, at least in my book, is the opposite. It's the sanctification of God's name." [85]

Rabbi Yitzhak Ginsburg is "one of the Lubovitcher sect's leading authorities on Jewish mysticism, the St. Louis born rabbi, who also has a degree in mathematics, speaks freely of Jews' genetic-based, spiritual superiority over non-Jews."[86]

Ginsburg told *Jewish Week,* "If a Jew needs a liver, can you take the liver of an innocent non-Jew passing by to save him? The Torah would probably permit that. Jewish life has an infinite value. There is something infinitely more holy and unique about Jewish life than non-Jewish life." [87]

Rabbi Ginsburg also has declared, "We have to recognize that Jewish blood and the blood of a *goy* are not the same thing."[88]

Talmudic Doctrine: Non-Jews are not Human

The Talmud specifically defines all who are not Jews as non-human animals, and specifically dehumanizes Gentiles as not being descendants of Adam. Here are some of the Talmud passages which relate to this topic.

Kerithoth 6b: Uses of Oil of Anointing. "Our Rabbis have taught: He who pours the oil of anointing over cattle or vessels is not guilty; if over gentiles (goyim) or the dead, he is not guilty. The law relating to cattle and vessels is

---

[84]Sanhedrin 58b.

[85]*NY Times,* March 4, 1994, p. 10.

[86]*Jewish Week* (New York), April 26, 1996.

[87]Ibid.

[88]*NY Times,* June 6, 1989, p.5.

right, for it is written: "Upon the flesh of man (Adam), shall it not be poured (Exodus 30:32]); and cattle and vessels are not man (Adam).

"Also with regard to the dead, [it is plausible] that he is exempt, since after death one is called corpse and not a man (Adam). But why is one exempt in the case of gentiles (goyim); are they not in the category of man (Adam)? No, it is written: 'And ye my sheep, the sheep of my pasture, are man" (Adam); [Ezekiel 34:31]: Ye are called man (Adam) but gentiles (goyim) are not called man (Adam)."

In the preceding passage, the rabbis are discussing the portion of the Mosaic law which forbids applying the holy oil to men.

The Talmud states that it is not a sin to apply the holy oil to Gentiles, because Gentiles are not human beings (i.e. are not of Adam).

Another example from tractate Yebamoth 61a: "It was taught: And so did R. Simeon ben Yohai state (61a) that the graves of gentiles (goyim) do not impart levitical uncleanness by an *ohel* [standing or bending over a grave], for it is said, 'And ye my sheep the sheep of my pasture, are men (Adam), [Ezekiel 34:31]; you are called men (Adam) but the idolaters are not called men (Adam)."

The Old Testament Mosaic law states that touching a human corpse or the grave of a human imparts uncleanness to those who touch it. But the Talmud teaches that if a Jew touches the grave of a Gentile, the Jew is *not* rendered unclean, since Gentiles are not human (not of Adam).

From Baba Mezia 114b: ""A Jewish priest was standing in a graveyard. When asked why he was standing there in apparent violation of the Mosaic law, he replied that it was permissible, since the law only prohibits Jews from coming into contact with the graves of humans (Adamites), and he was standing in a gentile graveyard. For it has been taught by Rabbi Simon ben Yohai: 'The graves of gentiles [goyim] do not defile. For it is written, 'And ye my flock, the flock of my pastures, are men (Adam)' (Ezekiel 34:31); only ye are designated men (Adam)."

Ezekiel 34:31 is the alleged Biblical proof text repeatedly cited in the preceding three Talmud passages. But Ezekiel

34:31 does not in fact support the Talmudic notion that only Israelites are human. What these rabbinical, anti-Gentile racists and ideologues have done in asserting the preceding absurdities about Gentiles is distort an Old Testament passage in order to justify their bigotry.

In Berakoth 58a the Talmud uses Ezekiel 23:20 as proof of the sub-human status of gentiles. It also teaches that anyone (even a Jewish man) who reveals this Talmudic teaching about non-Jews deserves death, since revealing it makes Gentiles wrathful and causes the repression of Judaism.

The Talmudic citation of this scripture from Ezekiel as a "proof-text" is specious, since the passage does not prove that Gentiles are animals. The passage from Ezekiel only says that some Egyptians had large genital organs and copious emissions. This does not in any way prove or even connote that the Egyptians being referred to in the Bible were considered animals. Once again, the Talmud has falsified the Bible by means of distorted interpretation.

Other Talmud passages which expound on Ezekiel 23:20 in this racist fashion are: Arakin 19b, Berakoth 25b, Niddah 45a, Shabbath 150a, Yebamoth 98a. Moreover, the original text of Sanhedrin 37a applies God's approval only to the saving of Jewish lives (cf. the *Hesronot Ha-shas*, Cracow, 1894).

The Kol Nidrei Nullification of Vows

One of the most sensitive portions of Jewish ritual which has been the object of a certain amount of informed protest and exposure by Gentiles over the centuries[89] is the Kol Nidrei rite of Yom Kippur, which entails the nullification of all vows made in the coming year.

Almost all stories about this rite which appear annually, around September, in establishment newspapers and other media, invariably falsify it, describing it as a noble plea for forgiveness and "atonement" for *having broken promises in the past,* which, if that were the case, would indeed be

[89]For example, the poet Samuel Butler in *Hudibras* (1662).

a commendable exercise. But as is customary in Judaism, the official explanation intended for the goyim is deceiving.

Historian William N. Grimstad writes: "British Hebraist Alexander McCaul was eloquent in his protest at the potentially socially devastating attitude inculcated by rabbinic Judaism, that oaths and solemn undertakings to Goyim can be cavalierly broken...the primary synagogue ritual dealing with it, the famous *Kol Nidrei*...is held as part of the new year's observance each autumn, where it begins the evening service of *Yom Kippur*..." [90]

The Talmudic law concerning the Kol Nidrei rite is as follows: "And he who desires that none of his vows made during the year shall be valid, let him stand at the beginning of the year and declare, 'Every vow which I make in the future shall be null.'"[91]

The reader will note that this Talmud passage declares that the action nullifying vows is to be taken *at the beginning of the year* and with regard to promises made *in the future.*

This distinction is critical since it contradicts what the deceivers claim is a humble, penitential rite of begging forgiveness for promises broken in the past, rather than what it is, a nullification made in advance for vows and oaths yet to be made (and deliberately broken with impunity).

"...the *Kol Nidrei* is without doubt one of the three most hateful and, for non-Jews, fateful elements of Jewish law and practice (along with the imputations to us of inherent moral turpitude and illegitimacy, and thinly veiled sanctions of murder)...This is so not only because it declares open season upon unsuspecting non-Jews for officially sanctioned yet covert deceptive practice, but worse, for the combined attitude of personal contempt for us gullible 'marks,' and inevitable moral abasement that this sort of

[90]William N. Grimstad, *Talk About Hate* [Colorado Springs, Colorado: Council on Hate Crime, 1999], p. 254.

[91]Nedarim 23a and b. The Talmud admits there is no Biblical warrant for the Kol Nidrei. Cf. Hagigah 1:8.

treachery fosters in its practitioners." [92]

The Kol Nidrei rite "...is popularly regarded as the most 'holy' and solemn occasion of the Jewish liturgical year, attended even by many Jews who are far from religion..."[93]

The popularity of Kol Nidrei is no wonder since it allows Jewish participants to be absolved, in advance, of all contracts, vows and oaths they make and then break in the coming new year. This corresponds to the Talmudic lesson that God rewards clever liars (Kallah 51a), and it testifies to the fact that Judaism would seem to be more of a crime syndicate than a religion.

Moses Maimonides:
Advocate of Extermination

The rabbinic teacher Moses Maimonides ("Rambam"), is revered in Judaism as a supreme "sage" of the highest stature.

"Moses Maimonides is considered the greatest codifier and philosopher in Jewish history. He is often affectionately referred to as the Rambam, after the initials of his name and title, Rabenu Moshe Ben Maimon, "Our Rabbi, Moses son of Maimon." [94]

According to the introduction to the book, Maimonides' *Principles,* p. 5, Maimonides "spent twelve years extracting every decision and law from the Talmud, and arranging them all into 14 systematic volumes. The work was finally completed in 1180, and was called Mishnah Torah, or "Code of the Torah."

Here is what Maimonides taught concerning saving people's lives, especially concerning saving the lives of Gentiles and Christians, or even Jews who dared to deny the "divine inspiration" of the Talmud:

"Accordingly, if we see an idolater (gentile) being swept away or drowning in the river, we should not help him. If

---

[92]Grimstad, op. cit., p. 255.

[93]Shahak, op. cit., p. 48.

[94]*Maimonides' Principles*, edited by Aryeh Kaplan, Union of Orthodox Jewish Congregations of America, p. 3. I am indebted to Alan R. Critchley for unearthing this material.

we see that his life is in danger, we should not save him."[95]

The Hebrew text of the Feldheim 1981 edition of *Mishnah Torah* states this as well.

In his writings Maimonides taught that Christians should be exterminated. Immediately after Maimonides' admonition that it is a duty for Jews not to save a drowning or perishing Gentile, he informs us of the Talmudic duty of Jews towards Christians, and also towards Jews who deny the Talmud. Maimonides, *Mishnah Torah*, (Chapter 10), p. 184:

"It is a mitzvah [religious duty], however, to eradicate Jewish traitors, minim, and apikorsim, and to cause them to descend to the pit of destruction, since they cause difficulty to the Jews and sway the people away from God, as did Jesus of Nazareth and his students, and Tzadok, Baithos, and their students. May the name of the wicked rot."

The Jewish publisher's commentary accompanying the preceding teaching of Maimonides, states that Jesus was an example of a *min* (plural: *minim*). The commentary also states that the "students of Tzadok" were defined as those Jews who deny the truth of the Talmud and who uphold only the written law (i.e. the Old Testament).

Maimonides taught in another part of the Mishnah Torah that Gentiles are not human:

"Man alone, and not vessels, can contract uncleanness by carriage. ...The corpse of a gentile, however, does not convey uncleanness by overshadowing. ...a gentile does not contract corpse uncleanness; and if a gentile touches, carries, or overshadows a corpse he is as one who did not touch it. To what is this like? It is like a beast which touches a corpse or overshadows it. And this applies not to corpse uncleanness only but to any other kind of uncleanness: neither gentiles nor cattle are susceptible to

---

[95]Maimonides, *Mishnah Torah*, (Moznaim Publishing Corporation, Brooklyn, New York, 1990, Chapter 10, English Translation), p. 184.

any uncleanness." [96]

Maimonides: Premiere Anti-Black Racist

The perplexing problem of what to do with the savage anti-black pronouncements of the rabbi hailed as one of *the* greatest Jewish thinkers of all time has been a difficult one for his acolytes. When in doubt the usual policy has been to falsify his texts, bowdlerizing and sanitizing them.

The first English-language translation of Maimonides' famous *Guide of the Perplexed* was completed in 1881 by M. Friedlander, PhD. A second edition was prepared in 1904. A Rev. H. Gollancz is credited with translating some parts of the first twenty five chapters. However our concern here is with the remaining 29 chapters translated by Friedlander himself; specifically chapter 51.

Before commencing our scrutiny it should be noted that Maimonides' *Guide of the Perplexed* has become a classic among Gentile Judeophiles who pride themselves on their humanist and progressive credentials.

Largely thanks to the Friedlander translation, which was published for popular consumption in an inexpensive, mass market printing (Friedlander called it a "cheap edition"), it has entered the Western canon as a paradigm of lofty rabbinic philosophy, on par with Aristotle, Augustine and Aquinas as worthy of study, application and emulation by those seeking genuine enlightenment. [97]

The Jewish translator Dr. Friedlander and his backers

---

[96]*The Code of Maimonides*, vol. 10, translated by Herbert Danby, Yale University Press, New Haven, 1954, pp. 8-9.

[97]The Jesuit Malachi Martin was much enamored of Maimonides. He told *The New American* magazine (June 9, 1997, p. 41), that he intended to write a similar book: "In the 12th century, the Jewish scholar Maimonides wrote a *Guide for the Perplexed* for his people. I hope to write a book somewhat like his to help Catholics..." Martin was instrumental in the promulgation of *Nostra Aetate*, the Vatican document absolving the Jews of the murder of Jesus. He gave an inside view of this historic reversal in an article he wrote for the American Jewish Committee under the pseudonym, F.E. Cartus: "Vatican II & the Jews," *Commentary*, Jan. 1965.

knew that in Maimonides' *Guide of the Perplexed* there were racist Talmudic teachings about black people, e.g. that they are a sub-human species, above simian but below human.

Here is how Friedlander translated the problem passage in his popular version intended for the masses:

"The people who are abroad are all those that have no religion, neither one based on speculation nor one received by tradition.. Such are the extreme Turks that wander about in the north, the Kushites who live in the south, and those in our country who are like these. I consider these as irrational beings, and not as human beings, they are below mankind, but above monkeys, since they have the form and shape of man and a mental faculty above that of a monkey."[98]

But this is what Maimonides actually wrote, as published in a translation intended mainly for scholars:

"Those who are outside the city are all human individuals who have no doctrinal belief, neither one based on speculation nor one that accepts the authority of tradition: such individuals as the furthermost Turks found in the remote North, the Negroes found in the remote South, and those who resemble them that are with us in these climes. The status of those is like that of irrational animals. To my mind they do not have the rank of men, but have among the beings a rank lower than the rank of man but higher than the rank of apes. For they have the external shape and lineaments of a man and a faculty of discernment that is superior to that of the apes." [99]

It would be difficult to assess the degree of oppression which this Talmudic passage, as codified by Maimonides, as well as another Talmudic passage we shall examine,

---

[98]Moses Maimonides, *The Guide for the Perplexed,* translated by M. Friedlander, [New York: Dover Publications, 1956), ch. 51, p. 384.

[99]Moses Maimonides, *The Guide of the Perplexed* [Moreh Nevuk'him], translated by Shlomo Pines [Chicago: University of Chicago Press, 1963], vol. 2, pp. 618-619.

has created for the black race. [100]

Moreover, the process of dissimulation through the substitution of code words (Kush for Negro here, and Kush for goy in the Soncino edition of the Talmud) is a feature of numerous texts of the religion of Judaism.

The most famous source of anti-Negro bigotry in the West, often mistakenly attributed to the Bible, centers on the story of Ham and Noah's cursing of Canaan.

The Biblical curse of enslavement in Genesis 9 has no specific racial identification and contains no anti-black bigotry. Jewish scholar Harold Brackman in his 1977 Ph.D. dissertation indicates that the source of the racial taint attached to Ham and his son Canaan and their descendants, is the Talmud, not the Bible:

"There is no denying that the Babylonian Talmud was the first source to read a Negrophobic content into the episode...The Talmudic glosses of the episode added the stigma of blackness to the fate of enslavement that Noah predicted for Ham's progeny."[101]

Christians who pay the Talmud no heed will not espouse its erroneous identification of the African race with Bible-sanctioned enslavement. But Christians who over the centuries have conceded some authority to the "Talmudic glosses" which *added* the stigma of blackness" to the account in Genesis 9, will -- as in so many other instances where the Talmud is heeded -- fall into a pit of bigotry and falsehood having no Scriptural basis.

Brackman quotes the Talmud's version of Genesis 9:

"Ham is told by his outraged father that, because you

---

[100]Cf. *The Secret Relationship Between Blacks and Jews Volume One* [Boston: Historical Research Department, 1994]. ISBN: 0-9636877-0-0. The Talmud also posits a demonic species of human descended from Cain as a result of supposed sexual intercourse between Eve and Satan. Cf. Ted R. Weiland, *Eve: Did She or Didn't She?* [Scottsbluff, Nebraska: Mission to Israel Ministries, 2000], pp. 94-103.

[101]Harold Brackman, "The Ebb and Flow of Conflict: A History of Black-Jewish Relations Through 1900" (1977 Ph.D. dissertation), pp. 79-81.

have abused me in the darkness of the night, your children shall be born black and ugly; because you have twisted your head to cause me embarrassment, they shall have kinky hair and red eyes; because your lips jested at my expense, theirs shall swell."[102]

The Schindler's List Quote

The Babylonian Talmud's text in Sanhedrin 37a restricts the duty to save life to saving only Jewish lives.

The book on Hebrew censorship, (*Hesronot Ha-shas*), notes that some Talmud texts use a universalist phrasing:

"Whoever destroys the life of a single human being...it is as if he had destroyed an entire world; and whoever preserves the life of a single human being ...it is as if he had preserved an entire world."

However, *Hesronot Ha-shas* points out that this is not the authentic text of the Talmud.

In other words, the preceding universalist rendering is a counterfeit and thus, for example, this universalist version, which Steven Spielberg in his famous movie, *Schindler's List* attributed to the Talmud (and which became the motto of the movie on posters and in advertisements), is a hoax and constitutes propaganda intended to give a humanistic gloss to a Talmud which, in its essence, constitutes racist hate literature.

In the authentic, original Talmud text it states that "whoever preserves *a single soul of Israel*, it is as if he had preserved an entire world" (emphasis supplied). The

---

[102]Ibid., p. 81. After his statements were cited by a prominent black leader, Brackman denied that his dissertation argued that the Talmud espoused anti-black racism. However, Jewish scholar Lenni Brenner refuted the denial by quoting Brackman's own descriptions of the anti-black passages in the Talmud. Cf. Brenner, *N.Y. Times,* Feb. 28, 1994, p. 16. Also cf. I. Epstein et al., trans. *The Babylonian Talmud,* 35 vols. [London: Soncino, 1935-1948], Sanhedrin, II, 745. The Kabbalah also contains anti-black hatred: cf. Harry Sperling and Maurice Simon, trans., *The Zohar,* 5 vols. (London, 1931), vol. I, pp. 246-247.

authentic Talmud text sanctions only the saving of Jewish lives. Mr. Spielberg suppressed the actual Talmudic saying in favor of a fanciful version more suitable to the indoctrination he intended to impart to his audience.

Non-Jews are "Supernal Refuse"

Moreover, not only blacks and Christians, but Gentiles of all races are regarded as "supernal refuse" (garbage) by Talmud teachers such as the "towering sage" and founder of Chabad-Lubavitch, Rabbi Shneur Zalman.

This was analyzed in the Jewish magazine, *New Republic*:

"...there are some powerful ironies in Habad's new messianic universalism, in its mission to the gentiles; and surely the most unpleasant of them concerns Habad's otherwise undisguised and even racial contempt for the goyim.

"...medieval Jewish theologians--most notably the poet and philosopher Judah Ha-Levi in twelfth-century Spain and the mystic Judah Loew in sixteenth-century Prague--sought to define the Jewish distinction racially rather than spiritually...this...view, according to which there is something innately superior about the Jews, was rehabilitated in its most extreme form by Shneur Zalman of Lyady.

"The founder of Lubavitcher Hasidism taught that there is a difference of essence between the souls of Jews and the souls of gentiles, that only in the Jewish soul does there reside a spark of divine vitality."

"...Moreover, this characterization of gentiles as being inherently evil, as being spiritually as well as biologically inferior to Jews, has not in any way been revised in later Habad writing."[103]

Dr. Roman A. Foxbrunner of Harvard University quotes the founder of the Lubavitch Hasidim, Rabbi Zalman, as follows:

"Gentile souls are of a completely different and inferior order. They are totally evil, with no redeeming qualities whatsoever...Their material abundance derives from

---

[103] *The New Republic*, May 4, 1992.

supernal refuse. Indeed, they themselves derive from refuse, which is why they are more numerous than the Jews..." According to Rabbi Zalman, "All Jews were innately good, all gentiles innately evil...For RSZ (Rabbi Shneur Zalman) the kabbalist...gentiles were simply the embodiment of the kelipot..." [104]

Foxbrunner's quotations are from the works of Rabbi Zalman, whose masterwork was *Likutei Amarim Tanya,* or simply *Tanya.* The authoritative English-language version of this work was published in 1973 and reissued in 1984 by the Jewish "Kehot' Publication Society."

In chapter 19 of *Tanya,* Rabbi Zalman defines the Kabbalistic term, *kelipah* (also spelled as *kelipot* and *kelippot*): "...*kelipah*...wherefrom are derived the souls of the gentiles."

In *Tanya* chapter 10 (p. 948), Rabbi Zalman states that *kelipot* and another name for the condition which a Gentile represents, *sitra ahra,* "...are synonymous (with)...evil and impurity."

"...the three *kelipot* which are altogether unclean and evil containing no good whatever...From them flow and derive the souls of all the nations of the world." (Rabbi Zalman, ch. 6).

The foundational teachings of Judaism do not regard these "nations of the world" as human, as being "mankind." Only a "Jew" is a man: "The candle of G-d is the soul (*neshamah*) of man. What it means is that the souls of Jews are called 'man." (Rabbi Zalman, ch. 19).

According to the Kabbalistic *Zohar,* the *kelipot* are:

"...shells or husks of evil...waste matter...bad blood...foul waters...dross...dregs...the root of evil...It is in the book of the Zohar that we read for the first time of a twofold though corresponding division of souls into non-Jewish and Jewish.

"The first group has its source in the 'other side' or *sitra ahra,* the second in the 'holy side'...Interest in the Zohar is almost entirely confined to the psychic structure of the

---

[104] *Habad: The Hasidism of Shneur Zalman of Lyady,* [Northvale, New Jersey, Jason Aronson, Inc., 1993], pp. 108-109.

Jew. In the later Kabbalah...this duality between the 'divine soul' (*ha-nefesh ha-elohit*) and the 'natural soul' (*ha-nefesh ha-tiv'it*) is given enormous emphasis." [105]

Deception and Dissimulation in Judaism

The response of the orthodox rabbis to documentation regarding the racism and hatred in their sacred texts is simply to brazenly lie, in keeping with the Talmud's Baba Kamma 113a which states that Jews may use lies ("subterfuge") to circumvent a Gentile.

The Simon Wiesenthal Center, a multi-million dollar rabbinical propaganda center dispatched Rabbi Daniel Landes in 1995 to deny that the Talmud dehumanizes non-Jews. "This is utter rot," he said. His proof? Why, his word, of course.

Lying to "circumvent a Gentile" has a long patrimony in Judaism. Take for example the 13th century Talmud debate in Paris between Nicholas of Donin, a Jewish convert to Christianity, whom Hyam Maccoby admits had "a good knowledge of the Talmud"[106] and Rabbi Yehiel. Yehiel was not under threat of death, bodily injury, imprisonment or fine. Yet he brazenly lied during the course of the debate.

When asked by Donin whether there were attacks on Jesus in the Talmud, Yehiel denied that there were any. Donin, a Hebrew and Aramaic scholar, knew this to be false. Hyam Maccoby, a 20th century Jewish commentator on the debate, defends Rabbi Yehiel's lying in this way:

"The question may be asked, however, whether Yehiel really believed that Jesus was not mentioned in the Talmud, or whether he put this forward as an ingenious ploy in the desperate situation in which he found himself...It would certainly have been pardonable of the rabbi to attempt some condonation in which he did not fully believe, to prevent such tyrannical proceedings by one religious

---

[105]Gershom Scholem, *Kabbalah,* [op. cit.], pp. 125, 139, 156-157.

[106]Maccoby, op. cit., p. 26.

culture against another." [107]

This is how Jewish denial of the existence of hateful Talmud texts is justified to this day. A fanciful word for Jewish lying is conjured ("condonation") and deemed "pardonable," while any scrutiny of Jewish holy books by Christian investigators is characterized as a "tyrannical proceeding."

In 1994, Rabbi Tzvi Marx, director of Applied Education at the Shalom Hartman Institute in Jerusalem, made a remarkable admission concerning how Jewish rabbis in the past have issued two sets of texts: the authentic Talmudic texts with which they instruct their own youth in the Talmud schools (yeshiviot) and "censured and amended" versions which they disseminate to gullible non-Jews for public consumption.

Rabbi Marx states that in the version of Maimonides' teachings published for public consumption, Maimonides is made to say that whoever kills a human being transgresses the law.

But, Rabbi Marx points out "...this only reflects the censured and amended printed text, whereas the original manuscripts have it only as 'whoever kills an Israelite.'"[108]

The Jewish book, *Hesronot Ha-shas* ("that which is removed from the Talmud"), is important in this regard.[109]

Hesronot Ha-shas was reprinted in 1989 by Sinai Publishing of Tel-Aviv. *Hesronot Ha-shas* is valuable because it lists both the original Talmud texts that were later changed or omitted, and the falsified texts cited for Gentile consumption as authentic.

Historian William Popper states: "It was not always that long passages...were censored...but often single words alone were omitted...Often, in these cases, another method of

---

[107]Ibid., p. 28.

[108]*Tikkun: A Bi-Monthly Jewish Critique*, May-June, 1994.

[109]Cf. William Popper, *The Censorship of Hebrew Books*, p. 59.

correction was used in place of omission--substitution." [110]

For example, the translators of the English Soncino version of the Talmud sometimes render the Hebrew word goyim (Gentiles) under any number of disguise words such as "heathen, Cuthean, Kushite, Egyptian, idolater" etc. But these are actually references to Gentiles (all non-Jews). Footnotes for certain passages in the Soncino Talmud translation state: "Cuthean (Samaritan) was here substituted for the original goy..."

The heirs of the Pharisees often deny the existence of the Talmud passages here cited, in order to brazenly claim that such passages are the "fabrications of anti-Semites."

In 1994, the 80 year old Lady Jane Birdwood was arrested and prosecuted in a criminal court in London, England for the "crime" of publishing in her pamphlet, *The Longest Hatred*, the truthful statement that the Talmud contains anti-Gentile and anti-Christian passages.[111]

In the course of her Orwellian thought-crime trial, which was ignored by the U.S. media, a rabbi was called as a prosecution witness. The rabbi proceeded to flatly deny that the Talmud contained anti-Gentile or anti-Christian passages and on the basis of the rabbi's "prestige," this elderly and ailing woman was sentenced to three months in jail and fined the equivalent of $1,000.

"Judeo-Christian" Response to the Talmud

Neither the modern popes or the modern heads of Protestantism, have ever insisted that the rabbis of Judaism repudiate, condemn or apologize for the nullification of Scripture in the Talmud or the Talmud's murderous hate for Jesus Christ and His mother, as well as for Christians and Gentiles; or the mountain of folly, filth and sanctioned criminality which is contained within it. On the contrary, these heads of Churchianity have urged Christians to obey, honor and support the followers of the

---

[110]Ibid., pp. 58-59.

[111]She was accused of violating the Public Order Act of 1986.

Talmud. Therefore, it should be obvious that these Catholic and Protestant leaders are the worst betrayers of Jesus Christ on earth today. (Matthew 23:13-15; I Thess. 2:14-16; Titus 1:14; Luke 3:8-9; Rev. 3:9).

U.S. Government Lays the
Groundwork for Talmudic Courts

"Our" government under Presidents Reagan, Bush and Clinton, has provided, under the euphemism of education (for example, House Joint Resolution 173 and Public Law 102-14), a groundwork for the establishment of Talmudic "courts of justice" to be administered by disciples of Shneur Zalman's Chabad successor, Rabbi Menachem Mendel Schneerson.

Maimonides ruled that it is a Jewish court -- or a court appointed by Jewish authority --that enforces obedience and passes judgment on Gentiles, as well as promulgating *legislation by court order* for that purpose. Maimonides further decreed that any non-Jewish nation "not subject to our jurisdiction" (*tahaht yadeinu*) will be the target of Jewish holy war.[112]

These courts are to be convened allegedly under the "Noahide Laws" (proscriptions against idolatry supposedly based on the covenant with Noah). The U.S. presidents and Congress urged the adoption of the "Noahide" Laws as interpreted by Chabad-Lubavitch Grand Rabbi Schneerson.

Prof. Easterly of the Southern University Law Center, a Jewish legal expert, has compared this Public law 102-14 to the "first rays of dawn" which "evidence the rising of a still unseen sun."

The *Jewish Encyclopedia* envisages a Noahide regime as a possible world order immediately preceding the universal reign of the Talmud.

It has to be understood that we are not dealing with the Noah of the Bible when the religion of Judaism refers to

---

[112]Hilkhot Melakhim 8:9-10; 10:11. Also cf. Gerald J. Blidstein, "Holy War in Maimonidean Law," in *Perspectives on Maimonides* [Oxford, England: Oxford Univ. Press, 1991].

"Noahide law," but the Noahide law as understood and interpreted by the absolute system of falsification that constitutes the Talmud.

Under the Talmud's counterfeit Noahide Laws, the worship of Jesus is forbidden under penalty of death, since such worship of Christ is condemned by Judaism as idolatry. Meanwhile various forms of incest are permitted under the Talmudic understanding of the Noahide code. [113]

Furthermore, all non-Jews would have the legal status of *ger toshav* (resident alien[114]), even in their own land; as for example in occupied Palestine where newly arrived Khazars from Russia have an automatic right to housing and citizenship, while two million Palestinian refugees who either fled or were expelled by the Israelis, are forbidden the right of return.

Resident alien status has been clearly delineated in scholarly articles in leading Jewish publications. For example, Hebrew University Professor Mordechai Nisan, basing his exposition on Maimonides, stated that a non-Jew permitted to reside in a land ruled by Jewish law "must accept paying a tax and suffering the humiliation of servitude."

If Gentiles refuse to live a life of inferiority, then this signals their rebellion and the unavoidable necessity of Jewish warfare against their very presence.[115]

At a symposium ("Is Autonomy for Resident Aliens Feasible?") organized by Israeli Minister of Education Shulamit Aloni, the Israeli Chief Rabbi Shlomo Goren repeated the Talmudic teaching on resident aliens: that Judaism forbids "granting any national rights" to them. He ruled that such "Autonomy is tantamount to a denial

[113]*Enziklopediya Talmudit,* note 1, pp. 351-352.

[114]Alan Unterman, *Dictionary of Jewish Lore and Legend* [London: Thames and Hudson, 1991], p. 148).

[115]Mordechai Nisan, *Kivunim* (official publication of the World Zionist Organization), August, 1984, pp. 151-156.

of the Jewish religion." [116]

American taxpayers' subsidy of the so-called "U.S. Holocaust Museum" in Washington, D.C., is yet another indicator of the gradual establishment of a Jewish state religion in the U.S. This "Holocaust museum" excludes any reference to holocausts perpetrated by Jewish Communists against Christians in Russia and Eastern Europe, from 1917 onward.

The focus of the museum is almost entirely on Jewish suffering. Holocausts perpetrated by Israelis against Arabs in Lebanon and Palestine since 1948 are nowhere to be found in the exhibits of the U.S. "Holocaust Museum," which functions more like a synagogue than a repository of objective historical information.

It is through the rapid emergence of this ostensibly secular but all-pervasive "Holocaustianity" -- whereby the religion of Judaism is gaining enormous power and influence as mankind's supreme ethos and the creed of God's Holy People.

Jewish Law Requires Christians be Executed

Israeli "Torah scholars" have ruled that: "The Torah maintains that the righteous of all nations have a place in the World to Come. But not all religious Gentiles earn eternal life by virtue of observing their religion...And while the Christians do generally accept the Hebrew Bible as truly from God, many of them (those who accept the so-called divinity of Jesus) are idolaters according to the Torah, punishable by death, and certainly will not enjoy the World to Come." [117]

---

[116]Nadav Shraggai, *Ha'aretz,* Oct. 14, 1992.

[117]Statement from the Israeli "Mechon-Mamre Torah Scholars," as it appeared on their website at http://www.mechon-mamre.org/jewfaq/gentiles.htm on June 26, 2000; 12 Hayyim Vital St., Jerusalem ("Mechon Mamre is a small group of Torah scholars in Israel...").

Molestation in the Synagogue

In spite of the Old Testament's capital proscription against
men lying with men (Leviticus 20:13), the Talmud nullifies
this Old Testament law. For example, in tractate
Kiddushin, Jewish bachelors are permitted to sleep
together while "wrapped in a single cloak."

This is permissible, the rabbis decree, because Jewish
males are beyond reproach when it comes to accusations
of sodomy. "The rabbis said to Rabbi Yehuda: 'Jews are
not to be suspected of *mishkav zachur* (intercourse with a
male)." But, as is often the case with the Talmud, the
reality is otherwise.

The following allegations were published in the Hebrew
language Israeli newspaper *Ha'aretz:*

"...for many years, (Talmud scribe) Yaakov Yitzhak
Brizel...sodomized ultra-Orthodox boys. The greatest rabbis knew
-- and did nothing...

"At the age of 11, Moisheleh, the strongest fellow in the talmud
torah (school for ultra-Orthodox boys), went up to Shaiya Brizel
and said to him: 'Kid, I want you know that your father is not the
holy man you think he is. He is a homo.' ...Brizel was a scion of
the Brizel family, which founded ...the mysterious organization
that imposes moral order on the ultra-Orthodox ghetto...

"Had the father, Yaakov Yitzhak Brizel ...contented himself with
homosexual relations with adults, it is reasonable to suppose that
we would never have heard his son's story.

"However, in his book, *The Silence of the Ultra-Orthodox,*[118]
published a few weeks ago, the son claims that for decades his
father...sodomized yeshiva students. He committed the act in empty
synagogues during the hours between prayers and in other places.

"The greatest of the ultra-Orthodox rabbis...like Rabbi Landau
and the halachic sage Shmuel Halevi Hausner of Bnei Brak, knew
and kept silent. The father was a Hasid heart and soul, and went to
a number of rebbes.... the twin brother of the rebbe from Rehovot,
the Rebbe of Kretschnif in Kiryat Gat, was happy to accept the
father among his followers. Ultimately, claims Brizel, it was not
easy for the Rebbe from Kiryat Gat to be picky when he could win
such a respected adherent.

"...The proud father with the look of an honored rebbe, who

[118]Published in the Israeli state in Hebrew.

observed all the commandments from the slightest to the most important, used to pray at a certain yeshiva with the young boys. There, claims Shaiya Brizel, he hunted his victims. When the head of the yeshiva discovered the true reason that the respected Torah scribe was praying fervently at his yeshiva, he did not contact the police...

"Before the publication of his book, Shaiya Brizel met with the yeshiva head. 'You are right that we covered up for him,' admitted the man. 'I and a few other rabbis...I was busy trying to calm things down and hushing up the affair so that it would not get publicized.'

"(The son) published the book using real names. His entire family and almost all the rabbis appear under their own names. Only the names of some of the localities and the head of the yeshiva are disguised. To protect himself from a legal point of view, Brizel held a series of conversations with members of his family and rabbis, in which he demanded explanations of why they had covered up for his father's misbehavior. He secretly recorded all these conversations, even with his mother.

"If I had written without the names it would have been fiction and this certainly did not suit me," he explained. 'I wanted things to change, for ultra-Orthodox society to know that it can attempt to hide things and be hidden, but even if it takes 30 years, a Golem will always rise up against its creator and reveal everything. In this case, I was the Golem.'

"When Rachel Brizel, the daughter of a good Bnei Brak family, married an arranged match from the glorious Brizel family, she had no idea that she was destroying her own life. After six months, she caught her husband having sex with another man. In that case, at least it was with an adult.

"Shaiya Brizel relates that some of the boys with whom his father had relations sent letters of complaint to their own fathers; in the discreet ultra-Orthodox society they had no one else to whom they could complain.

"When she read these letters, my mother went out of her mind,' writes Brizel. 'Every such letter made her want to demand a divorce. Again and again batteries of mediators, the Brizel rabbis, would show up, whose job it was to calm her down so that, heaven forbid, she would not destroy the good name of the Brizel family.

"They could live with the fact that one of their own had raped minors, but for them divorce was an impossible situation.'

"...Twice, once during prayers in a synagogue, and once during a Gemara (Talmud) study hour at Rabbi Eliezer Shach's Ponevezh

Judaism's Strange Gods

Yeshiva, ultra-Orthodox men who were strangers to him touched his (Shaiya Brizel's) sexual organ, presumably on the assumption that he followed in his father's footsteps. The first time, he made a fuss, only to discover that the only thing that interested the people there was to hush the whole thing up. The second time, he made do with a whispered warning to the man.

"Shaiya Brizel is now 36 and the father of three; he works as an accountant. His father, 65, was forced to leave home several years ago and return to his elderly parents' apartment. Shaiya wrote this book after a suicide attempt in June.

'For all those years I was half dead. For the past five years I have been getting psychological treatment. During my talks with the psychologist I decided that I was going to spew out all this ugliness in the form of a book.'

"He took into account that there would be violent reactions to the book...which only came out a few weeks ago...Brizel suffers from a serious heart defect, which could cause his death. As a way of protecting himself, he has deposited a letter with three lawyers that contains serious allegations about the Eda Haredit, and he has informed the relevant people.

"Recently, he has moved to a new apartment, and he lives in the National Religious sector of a mixed community of National Religious and ultra-Orthodox families. Naturally, he started praying at the only Hasidic synagogue in the settlement. After the book came out, associates of the local rebbe (rabbi) informed him that he was *persona non grata.*

"Ironically, this same rebbe had come to the area after being compelled to leave several other communities on suspicion of having sodomized his pupils. In ultra-Orthodox society, revealing that acts of sodomy have been committed is a far graver offense than committing them.

"On the day the book was published, Brizel met with the head of the Hachemei Lublin Yeshiva, Rabbi Avraham Vazner. 'He told me that publishing the book was a million times worse than what my father had done...'

"*Ha'aretz* has been unable to obtain a response from Rabbi Yaakov Yitzhak Brizel. At his parents' home, a woman replied: "We don't care. Shaiya is a liar and there is nothing more to be said."

"*Ha'aretz* also requested the Brizels' response through the Eda Haredit activist Yehuda Meshi- Zahav. By the time the article went to press, there was no response through this channel either.

"Several weeks ago the father responded to the women's magazine *La'isha,* saying that he would sue the publishers, which has not yet happened. It is unlikely that it will happen.

"Shaiya Brizel was ready to put off publication of the book, on condition that the family sue him in a rabbinical court, in which the affair would be aired. He has said that no one in the family was prepared to take up the challenge.

"In the conversation with *La'isha*, the father said that he was indeed a homosexual, 'But I have had treatment and today I am no longer like that. All this is behind me.'

"In reply to a question as to whether he had sexual relations with minors, he replied: 'Perhaps I will talk about that some other time.' He accused his son Shaiya of being 'the only one who is after me. He has destroyed my life...He wrote this only for the money. He wanted money from me...Because of him I separated from my wife.'

"Shaiya's sister, Rivka Hubert, spoke with great anger to the La'isha reporter about the fact that her brother had revealed the names of the persons involved, and declared: 'We deny everything it says in the book." [119]

Rabbis *are* God

The hubris that regards Shaiya Brizel's publication of an exposé of alleged sodomy in the synagogue, as "a million times worse" than the act of sodomy itself,[120] also leads the rabbis to declare that God spends part of his day studying their sayings in the Talmud: "The day is twelve hours long. During the first three, the Holy One, blessed be he, is engaged in the study of the Torah." (Avodah Zarah 3B).

In Bava Metzia 86a, Rabbi Nahmani is called to heaven to settle a debate between God and "the rest of the fellowship" and to teach God who is clean and who is not, since the rabbi is the foremost expert (greater than God)

---

[119]*Ha'aretz*, Feb. 1, 2000.

[120]Being an informer (*moisser*) is considered far worse than being a sodomite or a molester. When Philip Eli Cohen was convicted at England's Southwark Crown Court in the summer of 1990 of molesting a five year old girl, more than 100 Jews attacked the home of the girls' parents with bricks and iron bars, reviling them as *moissers* because they had dared to give evidence against Cohen.

on plagues and contamination: "For said Rabbah b. Nahmani, 'I am absolutely unique in my knowledge of the marks of skin disease that is unclean and in the rules of uncleanness...'"

According to Berakhot 6a-b. God wears phylacteries on which are inscribed praise for the Jewish people.

In Berakhot 7A God asks a rabbi for a rabbi's blessing.

Judaism *is* the Talmud

Rabbi Jacob Neusner:

"That sustained, systematic exposition, through one instance after another, of the right reading of the Torah in both its media comes to Israel now as in the past in a single document, the Talmud of Babylonia.

"That statement of fact describes the centrality of Talmud in the future curriculum of the Judaic intellect, the priority of the Talmud from the time of its closure in about 600 C.E. to the present time.

"For 'Judaism' is Rabbinic Judaism, and the Talmud of Babylonia is the authoritative statement of the Torah that Judaism embodies.

"The Talmud is the prism, receiving, refracting all light. To state the proposition in academic language: into that writing all prior canonical writings emerged; to it, all appeal is directed; upon it, all conclusions ultimately rest. In the language of Torah itself: study of the Torah begins, as a matter of simple, ubiquitous fact, in the Talmud.

"...In all times, places, and writings, other than those rejected as heretical, from then to now, the Talmud formed the starting point and the ending point, the alpha and the omega of truth; justify by appeal to the Talmud, rightly read, persuasively interpreted, and you make your point; disprove a proposition by reference to a statement of the Talmud and you demolish a counterpoint.

"In reading the written Torah itself, the Talmud's exegesis enjoys priority of place. Scripture rightly read reaches Israel in the Talmud (and related writings of Midrash); sound exegesis conforms to the facts of the Talmud...

"In all decisions of law that express theology in everyday action, the Talmud forms the final statement of the Torah, mediating Scripture's rules. Innovation of every kind, whether in the character of the spiritual life or in the practice of the faith in accord with its

Judaism's Strange Gods P. 81

norms, must find justification in the Talmud." [121]

"That is the power of this Judaism, which for as long time, and for the majority of practitioners of Rabbinic Judaism today, defines the normative, the classical, the authentic Torah: Rabbinic Judaism.

"That formulation of the theology of Rabbinic Judaism, which is to say, of the Torah, therefore constitutes the Talmud's re-presentation of the Torah...to know the Torah, we have to think in the way in which Torah teaches us to think. No prior document spells out that way, in massive, tedious, repetitive detail, case by case by case, as does the Talmud of Babylonia." [122]

Part Two: The Kabbalah

It is not for nothing that the authoritative edition of the Talmud is known as the *Babylonian* Talmud. As Christians misled by apostate preachers and popes are increasingly consulting rabbinical sources for a "pure" understanding of the Old Testament, they are unknowingly consulting the occult.

Judaism is the religion of the Pharisees and the patrimony of Babylon, from whence the Talmudic and Kabbalistic traditions of Judaism ultimately derive. Orthodox Judaism's other major sacred book, the Kabbalah, is filled with astrological teachings, fortune-telling, gematria, necromancy and demonology.

Christians might find it eye-opening to visit a Hasidic Jewish area during "Purim" and observe the grotesque cavorting. Though the Purim festival uses the Book of Esther as its supposed proof-text, in practice the Jewish celebration of Purim is little more than a pagan Bacchanal. [123]

Orthodox rabbis place curses, cast spells and imagine they have powers greater than God, derived from their

[121] Neusner, *Rabbinic Judaism*, op. cit. p. 205.

[122] Ibid., p. 209.

[123] Cf. "Superstitions said legacy from Jewish ancestors," *Canadian Jewish News*, Nov. 16, 1989, p. 58 and J. Trachtenberg, *Jewish Magic and Superstition* (1934).

study of the *Sefer Yezriah,* a book of Kabbalistic magic.

Other major Kabbalistic texts include the *Sefer ha-Bahr* and the *Zohar* or "Book of Splendor."

The *Sefer Yetzirah* teaches the methods of fortune-telling, numerology and astrology by means of contact with demons.

In a footnote to the Soncino edition Talmud, the rabbinic editor states concerning the origins of the *Sefer Yetzirah,* "The work was ascribed to Abraham, which fact indicates an old tradition, and the possible antiquity of the book itself. It has affinities with Babylonian, Egyptian, and Hellenic mysticism and its origin has been placed in the second century B.C.E., when such a combination of influences might be expected." [124]

According to the *Sefer Yetzira*'s modern publisher, the book: "...aid(s) the development of telekinetic and telepathic powers. These powers were meant to help initiates perform feats that outwardly appeared magical. The magical kabbalah...uses various signs, incantations...by which initiates could influence or alter natural events." [125]

The book's translator states: "...the signs of the Zodiac are associated with the twelve Hebrew lunar months...The assignment here approximates Western astrology, but is more accurate from a Kabbalistic viewpoint...Also associated with each of these twelve signs is a permutation of the names YHVH and Adony. By meditating on these combinations, as well as the derivative of the 42 Letter Name, one can gain knowledge of things that will happen in designated times...

"One of the most important factors in astrology is the time and date of a person's birth. The Talmud thus states that there is a 'Mazal of the hour.' The time, day and date upon which a person is born has an important influence on his destiny (Shabbat 156a). Elsewhere the Talmud teaches that there is an angel called Laylah that oversees

[124]I. Epstein et al., trans., *The Babylonian Talmud,* [[op. cit.], footnote 9 to Sanhedrin 65b.

[125]Statement of the Samuel Weiser Publishing Co., York, Maine., 1997.

birth. It is this angel that proclaims if the individual will be strong or weak, wise or foolish, rich or poor (Niddah 16b).

"...Another important opinion is that of the practical Kabbalists. They write that Teli is actually a place under the firmament of Vilon, and that it is inhabited by humanoid beings, which deport themselves in holiness and purity like angels. The divine mysteries are revealed to these beings, and they have the authority to reveal these things to mortal humans. Methods are also given whereby these beings can be contacted." [126]

The Kabbalah is a collection of books of black magic and rank superstition. It is the other Jewish wing of the oral tradition of the elders, claiming, like the Talmud, to be part of a secret teaching given to Moses at Sinai.

"Kabbalists claimed that their tradition had originally been given to Moses at Sinai...Many oral traditions were reworked in the Zohar...The influence of Kabbalah on exoteric Judaism was widespread, presenting Jews with a powerful set of mystical symbols...influencing halakah and giving magical practices respectability as elements of practical Kabbalah." [127]

Barry W. Holtz, director of research at the Jewish Theological Seminary of America writes: "...in our century, scholarly researchers have made clear the centrality of Kabbalah to the whole of Jewish religious consciousness."[128]

Jewish Professor Lawrence Fine of Indiana University describes the Zohar (the canonical text of Kabbalism) as:

"...a work of extraordinary quality which was to exert profound influence upon virtually all subsequent Jewish mystical creativity...the Zohar was studied with reverence,

[126]*Sefer Yetzirah,* translated by Aryeh Kaplan, (York, Maine: Samuel Weiser, 1997), pp. 171, 218, 223, 236-237.

[127]Alan Unterman, *Dictionary of Jewish Lore and Legend,* (op. cit.), p. 110. Unterman is an official of the Yeshurun Synagogue in Gatley, England.

[128]Barry W. Holtz, editor, *Back to the Sources: Reading the Classic Jewish Texts* [op. cit.], p. 26.

awe and intensity by Jews in the most diverse communities throughout the world." [129]

The earliest Kabbalistic book was the *Sefer ha-Bihar,* "a remarkable book insofar as it represented the emergence of a striking set of Gnostic motifs within the heart of rabbinic Judaism." [130]

"The Gnostic character of this cosmogony cannot be denied...Gnostic theology was able to dominate the mainstream of Jewish religious thought..." [131]

The first Gnostic is generally reputed to be Simon Magus: "Now for some time a man named Simon had practiced sorcery in the city and amazed all the people of Samaria. He boasted that he was the power of God that is called great." [132]

Because Simon offered to pay the apostles that he might acquire the Holy Spirit, his name became the eponymous basis for the sin of Simony.

"...the terms in which Simon is said to have spoken of himself are testified by the pagan writer Celsus to have been current with the pseudo-Messiahs still swarming in Phoenicia and Palestine at his time...It is of interest, though in a context far removed from ours, that in Latin surroundings Simon used the cognomen *Faustus* ('the favored one'): this in connection with his permanent cognomen 'the Magician...'" [133]

The Gnostic components of the religion of Judaism pertain to self-worship. This doctrine does not come from the Bible, which is filled with prophetic jeremiads against the Israelites for their faithlessness. According to Rabbi S.R.

---

[129] Lawrence Fine, "Kabbalistic Texts," *Back to the Sources: Reading the Classic Jewish Texts* [op. cit.], pp. 309 and 311.

[130] Ibid., p. 308.

[131] Gershom Scholem, *Kabbalah* [op. cit.], p. 143.

[132] Acts 8: 9-10.

[133] Hans Jonas, *The Gnostic Religion* [Boston: Beacon Press, 1963], pp. 103, 111.

Hirsch's key depiction of the Jewish man, unlike the rest of mankind, the Jew alone is imbued with the metaphysical qualities necessary for fulfilling divine destiny; Jews alone possess an innate disposition toward obeying God.[134]

The Kabbalah teaches that the presence of the divine (*Shekhinah*) in the world is exclusively due to the existence of the Jewish people

The oral traditions of the elders decree that the lifelong study of rabbinic tradition is not only a way to get closer to God, it is a way to become God. According to the Talmud, God himself is a student of the rabbis' tradition -- "he studies the Talmud three times a day." [135]

The traditions of Judaism were acquired from Babylon, but their original transmission point was Egypt:

"...there was abroad in the Hellenistic world gnostic thought and speculation entirely free of Christian connections...The Hermetic writings...(of) the *Poimandres* treatise...of the 'Thrice-greatest Hermes' originated in Hellenistic Egypt, where Hermes was identified with Toth...*Poimandres* is an outstanding document of gnostic cosmogony...according to which Man precedes creation and himself has a cosmogonic role. Rabbinical speculations about Adam based on the duplication of the report of his creation...referred to a celestial and terrestrial Adam respectively...

"Certain Zoroastrian teachings, either through the medium of Jewish speculations or directly, may also have contributed to the conception of this supremely important figure of gnostic theology. The departure from the biblical model...is conspicuous... The system of *Poimandres* is centered around the divine figure of Primal Man...the new bisexual creation..." [136]

The chief trait shared by Gnosticism and Kabbalism is a provenance of conceit and pride and a sub-rosa tradition

---

[134]S. Raphael Hirsch, *Nineteen Letters;* letter twelve.

[135]Avodah Zarah 3b.

[136]Hans Jonas, op. cit., pp. 147-155. In Kabbalah this bisexual creation is called Adam Kadmon.

of a superman with a hidden sexual aspect, that of a hermaphrodite.

This goes deeply into the "magical" work which both Jewish and Hermetic-Gnostic (and later Neo-platonic, alchemical, Rosicrucian and masonic) adepts performed behind a smokescreen of diversionary rhetoric.

Unfortunately, many naive students of Gnosticism have limited their research to the exoteric, philosophical Gnosticism intended for "profane" outsiders-- the dualism and hatred of matter attributed to the Gnostic offshoots, Manicheanism and Albigensianism. [137]

In medieval Spain, at Castile, the most prominent Gnostics were Jewish rabbis and Kabbalists such as Jacob Kohen, Moses ben Shemtov de Leon and Moses of Burgos. The prominent feature of their thinking was the development of an elaborate theory of a demonic emanation of ten *Sefirot*.

The Gnostic-Hermetic tradition finds resonance in the pages of the Kabbalistic text, *Sefer ha-Bahir* which had a profound influence on the Christians in the south of France, resulting in their susceptibility to Cathar/Albigensian demonology and "perfecti" Phariseeism. [138]

Kabbalism is imbued with a homicidal element by virtue of its legendary origin with Rabbi Simon ben Yohai who

---

[137]The Albigensians arose in the Provencal region of southern France at Languedoc, seedbed of the medieval Kabbalistic revival at the rabbinical court of Narbonne, circa 1160-1235. The most prominent figure in this revival was a Kabbalist steeped in Hermetic lore, Isaac the Blind, grandson-in-law of Abraham ben Isaac, the chief rabbi of the rabbinic court.

[138]For more on Albigensianism cf. Hoffman, *Secret Societies and Psychological Warfare.* For further study of the Gnostic and Hermetic in Judaism cf. Kalman Bland, "Neoplatonic and Gnostic Themes in Rabbi Moses Cordovero's Doctrine of Evil," *Bulletin of the Institute of Jewish Studies,* 1975, no. 3; and Isaiah Tishby (a.k.a. Yesaiah Tishbi), "Gnostic Doctrines in 16th Century Jewish Mysticism," *Journal of Jewish Studies,* 1955, no. 6.

"...according to traditional belief, (is) the author of the Zohar, the prime text of Jewish mysticism...just before his death in Galilee, he revealed to his students some of the greatest secrets of the Kabbalah."[139] As noted in the preceding section on the Talmud, Simon ben Yohai is the rabbi who proclaimed that "Even the best of the gentiles should all be killed."

The Kabbalah and its votaries exhibit at least the same degree of fanatical hostility toward non-Jews as does the Talmud.

"...a much revered Kabbalist of the 1500s (was) Isaac Luria, whose *Etz Chaim* ("tree of life") discusses the *olam ha-tohu* ("realm of confusion"--the subhuman non-Jewish world) and *olam ha-tikkun* ("realm of restoration"--the...paradisaical Zionist world empire to come)..." [140]

Kabbalah scholar Yesiah Tishbi quotes Rabbi Hayim Vital, the chief codifier of Rabbi Luria, who wrote in his book, *Gates of Holiness:*

"The Emanating Power, blessed be his name, wanted there to be some people on this low earth that would embody the four divine emanations. These people are the Jews, chosen to join together the four divine worlds here below."

Tishbi went on to further quote Vital's work in underscoring the Kabbalistic teaching of Isaac Luria that non-Jews are Satanic: "Souls of non-Jews come entirely from the female part of the Satanic sphere. For this reason souls of non-Jews are called evil..."[141]

The Messianic age of restoration and redemption (*tikkun olam*) forecast by the religion of Judaism and spoon-fed to their partisans among the goyim, posits a world restored to universal harmony and justice. That's the cover story,

---

[139]Samuel Heilman, *Defenders of the Faith,* [NY: Schocken Books, 1992] p. 118.

[140]Grimstad, op. cit., p. 252.

[141]Yesaiah Tishbi, *Torat ha-Rave-ha-Kelippah be-Kabbalat ha-Ari* ("The Theory of Evil and the Satanic Sphere in Kabbalah"); [1942; reprinted 1982].

anyway. The truth is somewhat more macabre, as the Jerusalem-based historian Yesiah Tishbi relates:

"...the presence of Israel among the nations mends the world, but not the nations of the world...it does not bring the nations closer to holiness, but rather extracts the holiness from them and thereby destroys their ability to exist...(T)he purpose of the full redemption is to destroy the vitality of all the peoples." [142]

Against Nature

The core of Judaism, like the core of Gnosticism and Egyptian Hermeticism, is magic, the manipulation of the universe, *contra* God's creation; i.e. against nature.

Gershom Scholem (1897-1982) was Professor of Kabbalah at Hebrew University in Jerusalem. He wrote that there is: "...in practical Kabbalah...a good deal of 'black' magic -- that is, magic...of various dark, demonic powers...Such black magic embraced a wide realm of demonology and various forms of sorcery that were designed to disrupt the natural order of things and to create illicit connections between things that were meant to be kept separate...In the *Tikkunei Zohar* the manipulation of such forces is considered justifiable under certain circumstances..." [143]

This diabolical element is rarely acknowledged. Judith Weill, a professor of Jewish mysticism in England and an adviser to London's Jewish Museum states: " The Bible quite clearly prohibits magic, so how come we have such a complex system? The answer is that magic is deeply rooted in Jewish tradition--but we don't call it magic." [144]

One of the most common and popular manifestations of Kabbalistic practice is the placing of curses and the use of good luck charms and other magical amulets--all by rabbis-- practices which are an abomination to the God of Israel.

In the Israeli state several rabbis specialize in the trade in magic amulets and charms, both in concocting them as

---

[142]Ibid., pp. 139-142.

[143]Gershom Scholem, *Kabbalah* [op. cit.], pp. 183-184.

[144]*Jewish Chronicle*, May 7, 1999.

well as disseminating them. Among these are the Moroccan-born "wonder" rabbi, "Baba Baruch" Abu-Hatzeria and the Iraqi-born Rabbi Yitzhak Kedouri.

During the 1996 Israeli elections, Rabbi Kedouri ordered his followers to vote for the Sephardic Shas party and he distributed "kabbalistic amulets" to those Israelis who promised to vote for Shas. These "good luck charms...swayed thousands of voters." [145]

Britain's leading Jewish newspaper, the *Jewish Chronicle,* further states that many of these occult practices are taught in Jerusalem at Yeshivat Hamekubalim, a rabbinic seminary noted for "specializing in the occult."

The sacred Kabbalistic handbook which gives instruction to the rabbis on the making of amulets, charms and talismans is the *Sefer Raziel:*

"...written around 1230 A.D. by Eleazer of Worms and drawing on Egyptian and Babylonian practices...Before use, amulets and incantations have to be tested and approved. The rabbi or kabbalist who gives his blessing can be blamed or lose his reputation if his charm does not work; conversely he gains kudos -- and a good income -- if his amulets or spells are effective."[146]

Allegedly, the most spectacularly successful Kabbalistic spell of modern times was the *Pulsa D'nura* ("whip of fire") curse which was placed on Israeli Prime Minister Yitzhak Rabin, who was returning land stolen from the Palestinians when he was assassinated. The "spell" was cast by ten Kabbalistic rabbis in front of Rabin's Jerusalem residence. [147]

"They intoned all sorts of ancient Jewish oaths, curses, and other voodoo-like incantations designed to bring about Rabin's death...Shortly afterward, by a strange coincidence, an international conference on 'Magic and Magia in

---

[145]*Jewish Chronicle,* Oct. 9, 1998.

[146]Helen Jacobus, "Eye Jinx," *Jewish Chronicle,* May 7, 1999.

[147]*Ma'ariv,* Nov. 6, 1995.

Judaism' took place in Jerusalem." [148]

Rabin had been labeled a *rodef,* a most pernicious category of Jewish traitor, by Israeli rabbis who also called him a Nazi and distributed retouched photos of Rabin in an SS uniform.

"An American rabbi named Avraham Hecht announced on Israeli television that Rabin deserved to die, invoking the authority of Maimonides." [149]

Rabin's assassin, Yigal Amir, was a student at Bar-Illan university, whose faculty included at the time Rabbi Israel Hess, author of a decidedly unlovely piece of hate propaganda entitled, *Mitzvat genocide batorah* ("The Commandment for Genocide in the Torah").

In his first appearance in court on Nov. 6, 1995, Amir stated:

"According to Jewish law, the minute a Jew betrays his people and country to the enemy he must be killed. No one taught me that law. I've been studying the Talmud all my life, and I have all the data." [150]

Star of Bohemia, Not David

The Israeli national talisman is the hexagram which is called the "star" of David and is supposed to be the ancient symbol of Israel. However, such an occult symbol is nowhere mentioned in the Bible.

It was "bequeathed" to Jewish leaders in the 14th century by the Hermeticist, King Charles IV of Bohemia and formally adopted as "the Star of David" in 1898 at the

---

[148]*NY Review of Books,* Dec. 21, 1995, p. 46.

[149]Ibid. According to reporter Eric J. Greenberg, Hecht, who is President of the Rabbinical Alliance of America, was a friend of New York Cardinal John O'Connor.

[150]NY Times, Nov. 27, 1995, p. 3. Amir's American supporters established a telephone hotline in NY to raise money for his defense. In two days more than $100,000 was collected. Cf. *Seattle Times,* Nov. 11, 1995, p. 4.

Second Zionist Congress in Switzerland. [151]

The original source of the symbol is androgynous, representing Adam Kadmon, the personification of the union of the male and female forces in one body. Kabbalistic doctrine brought the hexagram into Jewish tradition (a fact given official recognition by the Bohemian king).

Prof. Gershom Scholem wrote of how, within Judaism: "...amulets and protective charms can be found side by side with the invocation of demons, incantations...and even sexual magic and necromancy...As early as the geonic period the title *ba'al shem* or 'master of the name' signified a master of practical Kabbalah who was an expert at issuing amulets for various purposes, invoking angels or devils..."[152]

This demonic pantheon includes devils known in the Kabbalah as *shedim Yehuda'im.* Professor Scholem informs us that these devils are in submission to the Talmud.[153]

He writes: "...there are also good-natured devils who are prepared to help and do favors to men. This is supposed to be particularly true of those demons ruled by Ashmedai (Asmodeus) who accept the Torah and are considered 'Jewish demons.' Their existence is mentioned by the Hasidei Ashkenaz as well as in the Zohar." [154]

Elie Wiesel, the celebrated "sage of the Holocaust" who is widely feted in the Western media as a kind of lay

---

[151]W. Gunther Plaut, *The Magen David,* (1991). Because of its ubiquity as a universal symbol, the hexagram is occasionally found in some ancient Israelite funerary iconography. But to extrapolate from these relatively rare and minor instances, the supposition that this was Israel's national symbol is specious. It appears with equal or greater frequency in the iconography of many nations.

[152] Gershom Scholem, *Kabbalah* [op. cit.], p. 184.

[153]Ibid., p. 323. Scholem says these devils "submit to the Torah." To a Jewish scholar Torah signifies Talmud as well as Tanakh. Let us recall the doublespeak elucidated by Prof. Goldenberg: "Talmud *was* Torah. In a paradox...the Talmud was oral Torah in written form." (Goldenberg, op. cit., p. 166).

[154]Ibid., p. 322.

saint, has written an entire book praising these *ba'al* Kabbalists. Wiesel writes of: "...the great Rebbe Israel Baal Shem Tov, Master of the Good Name, known for his powers in heaven as well as on earth..."

In his account of the rabbi's exploits, Wiesel notes that God "...had to recognize the validity of Satan's arguments..." and that the rabbi's birth was a gift to his parents who "...had shown themselves hospitable and indulgent toward the Prophet Elijah, according to one version, and toward Satan, according to another."[155]

Like the Talmud, the Kabbalah supersedes, nullifies and ultimately replaces the Bible. Prof. Fine: "...the reader must become accustomed to regarding biblical language in a kabbalistically symbolic way. The Kabbalists taught that the Torah...is a vast body of symbols...The simple meaning of biblical language recedes into the background as symbolic discourse assumes control. The true meaning of Scripture becomes manifest only when it is read with the proper (sefirotic) code.

"Thus the Torah must not be read on the simple or obvious level of meaning; it must be read with the knowledge of a kabbalist who possesses the hermeneutical keys with which to unlock its *inner* truths." [156]

Jesus in the Kabbalah

The Kabbalah also exhibits the same potent hatred for Jesus as the sacred Jewish Talmud does, insulting Him in grotesque and reprehensible terms.

According to the most important Kabbalistic text, the Zohar, Jesus is a "dog" who resides amid filth and vermin:

"From the side of idolatry Shabbethaj (Saturn) is called Lilith, mixed dung, on account of the filth mixed from all kinds of dirt and worms, into which they throw dead dogs and dead asses, the sons of Esau and Ishmael, and there Jesus and Mohammed, who are dead dogs, are buried

[155]Elie Wiesel, *Souls on Fire: Portraits and Legends of Hasidic Masters* [NY: Random House, 1972], pp. 3 and 10.

[156]Lawrence Fine, "Kabbalistic Texts," *Back to the Sources: Reading the Classic Jewish Texts* [op. cit.], p. 337.

among them." [157]

This sick statement, the product of what can only be a diseased mind, comprises a portion of the same Kabbalah upheld and praised by "great Jewish humanists" such as Martin Buber and Elie Wiesel, and which is a focus of veneration among "progressive" elites in New Age circles and Hollywood. The perfidy and gross superstition embodied in the Kabbalah, one of the foundational texts of the religion of Judaism, testifies to the anti-Israel and anti-Biblical nature of this religion, since all such invocations of wicked spirit forces are an abomination to Yahweh.[158] Jerusalem's Hebrew University Professor of Kabbalah, Gershom Scholem:

"To the realm of practical Kabbalah also belong many traditions concerning the existence of a special archangelic alphabet, the earliest of which was 'the alphabet of Metatron.'..In Kabbalistic literature they are known as *eye writing* (ketav einayim) because their letters are always composed of lines and small circles that resemble eyes.

"...Such magical letters, which were mainly used in amulets, are the descendants of the magical characters that are found in theurgic Greek and Aramaic from the first centuries C.E. In all likelihood their originators imitated cuneiform writing that could still be seen in their surroundings, but which had become indecipherable and had therefore assumed magical properties...

"...practical Kabbalah did manifest an interest in the magical induction of the pneumatic powers of the stars through the agency of specific charms. The use of astrological talismans, which clearly derived from Arabic and Latin sources, is first encountered in the *Sefer ha-Levanah*...A number of kabbalistic works dealing with the preparation of magical rings combine astrological motifs with others taken from 'the science of combination.'

"...for the three-hundred-year period roughly from 1500 to 1800 (at the most conservative estimate) the Kabbalah was widely considered to be *the* true Jewish theology...Through the Diaspora, the number of (Jewish) folk customs whose origins were kabbalistic

[157] The Zohar III. 282a.

[158] Leviticus 19:31, 20:6, 27; Deuteronomy 18:10-12, I Samuel 15:23; I Chronicles 10:13-14; Psalm 5:4-6.

was enormous...Mystical and demonic motifs became particularly intertwined in the area of sexual life and practices to which an entire literature was devoted, starting with *Iggeret ha-Kodesh*...and continuing up to Nahman of Bratslav's *Tikkun ha-Kelali*....Similar ideas were behind the...*tikkun* of the *shoveim,* that is, of the demonic offspring of nocturnal emission.

"...This penetration of kabbalistic customs and beliefs, which left no corner of Jewish life untouched, is especially well-documented in...Isaiah Horowitz's *Shenei Luhot ha-Berit* (Amsterdam, 1648)...and the anonymous *Hemdat Yamim* (Izmir, 1731). [159]

Gematria

The primary process for Kabbalistic exegesis of the Bible is known as gematria, a Babylonian system of cryptography involving the use of letters to signify numbers. The first recorded use of gematria occurs in an inscription of Sargon II (727-707 B.C.).

Gematria is a form of numerology whereby the Hebrew "aleph-bet" (alphabet) is assigned numerical value. There are a multitude of various permutations and systems for arriving at the correct letter/word correspondence. One authority describes this complex esoteric Judaica thus:

"In the gematria *ketanah*, the value of each letter is its value in the primary gematria with any final zeros removed. Then there is classical gematria involving writing out the name of each letter and calculating the total from that. To the total of a word it is permissible to add a one, known as the kollel. Three transformations also are used: the Atbash, in which the first and last letters, the second and second to last, and so on, are exchanged; the Albam, which divides the aleph-bet into two parts of which the letters are exchanged; and the Ayak-Bachar, which is performed by dividing the letters into groups so that the letters of each have the same gematria ketanah."

Kabbalists regard the Bible as unintelligible without the mediation of complicated rabbinic rigmarole:

"...the sacred books, of which the keys are all kabbalistic from Genesis to the Apocalypse, have become so little intelligible to Christians, that prudent pastors have judged it necessary to forbid

---

[159]Scholem, op. cit., pp. 186-187, 190, 194-195.

them being read by the uninstructed among believers. Taken literally and understood materially, such books could be only an inconceivable tissue of absurdities and scandals...

"The ten Sephiroth and the twenty-two Tarots form what the Kabbalists term the thirty-two paths of absolute science...The rabbins also divided the Kabbalah into Bereshith, or universal Genesis, and Mercavah, or the Chariot of Ezekiel; then by means of a dual interpretation of the kabbalistic alphabets, they formed two sciences, called Gematria and Temurah, and so composed the Notary Art, which is fundamentally the complete science of the Tarot signs and their complex and varied application to the divination of all secrets..."[160]

The divinations being described in the preceding passage represent the stew of Babylonian superstition which the God of the Bible repeatedly excoriated and execrated. Yet it is this paganism which forms the central mystical system of the religion of Judaism for supposed "profound Biblical understanding."

Lest we imagine that the Kabbalah only has appeal to adherents of the religion of Judaism and occultists New Age or otherwise, we should recall the enthusiasm with which "Christians" greeted the 1997 publication of Michael Drosnin's *The Bible Code*. According to Drosnin's bestseller, the first five books of the Bible are written in a code which has been deciphered by rabbis who have discovered various prophecies of historical events and scientific discoveries hidden in the Pentateuch.

Here again is the fruit of the notion that only those using exegetical tools based upon the traditions of the elders of Judaism can plumb the Bible to its most profound depths.

Bible scholar James B. Jordan terms Drosnin's modern spin on the same old Babylonian superstition, "just another form of Qabbalism, this time with computers." Researcher David E. Thomas demolished the ridiculous and deceptive

---

[160]Eliphas Levi (a.k.a. Alphonse Louis Constant), *Dogme et Rituel de la Haute Magie* (1855-1856); trans. by Arthur E. Waite as *Transcendental Magic: Its Doctrine and Ritual*, [Great Britain: Tiger Books International, 1995], pp. 129 & 328.

claims in Drosnin's kabbalistic code. [161]

The idea that the Bible cannot be understood without the mediation of the rabbis of Judaism --without Talmudic explication, or in the case of Kabbalism, without the intervention of gematric numerology -- makes the Old and in some cases even the New Testament captive to the "traditions of the elders."

The pernicious fallacy of the religion of Judaism, that one can't truly know the Bible without commentary and interpretation from Talmudic and Kabbalistic rabbis and their traditions, is growing among "Christians," commensurate with the growing prestige of Judaism within Christendom. The acceptance of this deadly error effectively enables the enemies of the Bible to keep the teachings of Jesus from the common people to whom He had originally preached.

Instead, the rabbis, through their frontmen in the Church, mold and redirect "Christian" dogma based on interpretations of the Bible by the Pharisees of antiquity, further "clarified" by modern rabbinic pronouncements as filtered through the latest university theology seminars and trendy Church synods and councils acting as their mouthpieces.

This process is also abetted by supposed former adherents of Judaism who allegedly convert to Christianity and yet bring their Talmudic and Kabbalistic baggage with them into the Church, and attempt to baptize these traditions of theirs ("Messianic-Judaism") and present them to Christians as the "true" Christianity "practiced by Jesus" and withheld from the people as part of a conspiracy by

---

[161]David E. Thomas, "Hidden Messages and the Bible Code," *Skeptical Inquirer,* Nov./Dec. 1997, pp. 30-36. Christians are often gulled into this numerology partly from the desire to prove the validity of the Bible "scientifically." But fraud, whether in science or hermeneutics is never justified, and in the case of Kabbalistic gematria, casts the Biblical texts into even worse repute, as Thomas' investigative article demonstrates. To prove a truth with faulty methodology only compounds error.

wicked anti-semites and medieval inquisitors.[162]

During the Renaissance, crypto-Judaism formed the centerpiece of the occult belt of transmission which gave rise to Freemasonry and Rosicrucianism, the founders of which professed a "Christian Kabbalah" and performed their magic rites in the name of Jesus Christ.[163]

There is a substantial literature on this occult amalgam, including Frances A. Yates' classic studies, *The Rosicrucian Enlightenment* (1972) and *The Occult Philosophy in the Elizabethan Age* (1979.

The great appeal of the Kabbalah to nascent Freemasons and Roscicrucians was Judaism's doctrine, as expressed by Scottish Rite Freemason Albert Pike in his *Morals and Dogma*, of the "perfection" of the universe through the intervention of human brain power.

By this concept, God's creation is imperfect and the "Jew" and the Jew's assistant, the Freemason (an incomplete "Jew" as symbolized by the masonic square and compass, which is an incomplete hexagram, i.e. "Star of David"), will perfect this flawed creation.

This is expressed in the Talmud and Kabbalah. In the Talmud it appears in Sanhedrin 65b: "Rabbi Hanina and Rabbi Oshaia spent every Sabbath eve in studying the 'Book of Creation' by means of which they created a third-grown calf and ate it."

---

[162]These "converts" continue to engage in self-worship based on their supposed status as hereditary Israelites. They mock "replacement theology," claiming Christians will never replace the Jews as God's Chosen people. However, in this sense, no "replacement" occurred. It cannot be said that the good fig tree replaced the evil fig tree (Mat. 21:19), because the good fig tree had been there from the beginning. Christian Israel was comprised of Israelites, including Judeans ("Jews") who accepted Jesus; as well as converts from other nations who were grafted in; even as the evil fig tree of Judaism has had many converts.

[163]Occultists regard the Council of Trent (1545-1563), as a setback for their hopes for a Hermetic-Kabbalistic beachhead within the Roman Catholicism of that era; cf. *Gnosis Magazine,* Summer, 1990, p. 42.

The reference to the "Book of Creation" in Sanhedrin 65b, is to the Kabbalistic book of magic, the *Sefer Yetzirah,* which we discussed earlier.[164] The *Sefer Yetzirah* text is Judaism's pivotal thaumaturgic handbook for man playing God.

The notes to the Talmud passage Sanhedrin 65b in the Soncino edition state that the rabbis' magical act of creating the calf "does not come under the ban of witchcraft (because) the Creation was accomplished by means of the power inherent in...mystic combinations of the Divine Name." [165]

While this Talmudic reference to the rabbinic creation of life is obscure, another rabbinic act of creation using Kabbalistic combinations of the letters of the "Divine Name" is better known, if not notorious. This is the *golem*, dead matter supposed to have been brought to life as a Gentile-killing avenger. Kabbalistic legend has this occurring in the Bohemian capital city of Prague circa 1586, through the power of Rabbi Judah Loew, by means of a Kabbalistic amulet he fashioned containing magical letters.

This folklore, which has been invested with great significance by occultists within and without Judaism, is the original Frankenstein concept, which no longer seems so outlandish at the dawn of the 21st century with its animal and human cloning, its mixture of animal, human and insect genes and the subsequent growth of monstrous, hybrid creatures for the maximization of profit and under the pretext of finding "wonder cures" for various human ailments.

The rise of a city of death obsessed with autopsies, cadavers, fetal tissue and other dead matter, and with man playing God, was foretold in the writings of the Elizabethan mathematician, espionage agent, astrologer royal and founder of Freemasonry, Dr. John Dee.

Dee was a dedicated Kabbalist. He resided for several years in Prague at the height of Rabbi Judah Loew's

---

[164]See footnote 9 in the Soncino edition of Talmud Sanhedrin 65b [op. cit.].

[165]Ibid.

supposed golem rites and collaborated with him on behalf of his own masonic research, and in his capacity as agent of the espionage network headed by Sir Francis Walsingham and Sir William Cecil, the latter Queen Elizabeth I's minister of state. [166]

On June 27, 1589, while at Bremen, Germany, Dee was visited by Dr. Henricus Khunrath of Hamburg. Dee was a major influence on Khunrath's extraordinary symbolic occult work, "The Amphitheatre of Eternal Wisdom," an engraving with myriad cryptic occult symbols embedded within it.

"The engraving is a visual expression of the kind of outlook which Dee summed up in his *Monas hieroglyphica,* a combination of Cabalist, alchemical and mathematical disciplines through which the adept could achieve...a profound insight into nature...

"It could also serve as a visual expression of the leading themes of the Rosicrucian manifestos, Magia, Cabala,[167] and Alchymia united in an intensely religious outlook which included a religious approach to all the sciences of number."[168]

Dee is the first scientist in western history who can be definitively linked to a Satanic praxis based on the Kabbalah.

Kabbalistic philosophy was transmitted by Rabbi Judah Loew to Dee and from Dee to avant-garde scientists, mathematicians and theologians through a secret society, the Rosicrucians, which in the early 17th century mixed

---

[166]Frances A. Yates, *The Occult Philosophy in the Elizabethan Age* [London: Routledge and Keegan Paul, 1979] p. 87.

[167]"Cabala," the Italian rendering of the word Kabbalah, is sometimes used even by Jews. The Latinized spelling derives from the works of the Italian humanists, beginning with Pico della Mirandola. From cabala comes the English word for conspiracy, cabal. In Spanish, cabala signifies a card trick.

[168]Frances A. Yates, *The Rosicrucian Enlightenment* [Great Britain: Ark Paperbacks, 1986], pp. 38-39.

Protestant terminology with praise for the Kabbalah.

The Rosicrucian fraternity was under the protection and patronage of certain powerful aristocrats and rulers, including the Elector Palatine, Frederick V, King of Bohemia, who was the head of the Protestant Union.

This Bohemian Protestantism "...was an expression of a religious movement which had been gathering force for many years, fostered by secret influences moving in Europe, a movement toward solving religious problems along mystical lines suggested by Hermetic and Cabalistic influences." [169]

The Rosicrucian appeal in this vein was two-fold. It was crafted to persuade devoutly evangelical Protestants of the divinity of Judaism as manifested in the Kabbalah, and to convince scientists and intellectuals of the Kabbalah's potential as a key to the godhood of man and the "perfection" of divine creation by the intervention of human brain power.[170]

For example, the Rosicrucian manifesto of 1614, *The Fama,* links the Kabbalah with men "imbued with great wisdom," who "renew and reduce all arts to perfection so that man might thereby understand his own nobleness and how far his knowledge extendeth into Nature."

The manifesto relates that of "Magia and Cabala" the master of the Rosicrucians "makes good use." [171]

---

[169]Ibid., p. 40.

[170]"Protestants" and "scientists" in this context is not intended to suggest a modern dichotomy of religionists vs. atheists. In 17th century Europe most scientists were Christians. The infiltration of the Kabbalah was conducted under the auspices of intense piety and aspiration towards God, combined with a complex magical-scientific striving, a legacy of a Renaissance conception of the sciences in terms of "Magia," "Alchymia" and Kabbalah. In the 18th century, after the Kabbalah gained a firm purchase among the intelligentsia, its vehicle would be the insipid ecumenical monotheism and nominal Protestantism of Freemasonry.

[171]Yates, op. cit, pp. 238-240.

Dr. Dee's role in this context was pivotal:

"The...Rosicrucian manifesto, *The Confessio* of 1615, has published with it a tract in Latin called 'A Brief Consideration of a More Secret Philosophy.'

"This 'Brief Consideration' is based on John Dee's *Monas hieroglyphica,* much of it being word for word quotation from the *Monas.* Thus it becomes evident that the 'more secret philosophy' behind the manifestos was the philosophy of John Dee...the Rosicrucian movement in Germany was the delayed result of Dee's mission in Bohemia 20 years earlier..."[172]

And what was this secret philosophy?

It was the unmistakable rabbinic doctrine, expressed in the Kabbalistic texts as *tikkun olam* ("repair of the world") whereby Jewish (or Judaized) man assumes God-like powers to "correct" an "imperfect" and "flawed" Creation.[173]

Here too is the central contradiction in this doctrine, for it nearly always advertises itself to its *Novus Ordo* and Judeo-Christian percipients as a means for achieving healing, harmony, tranquility, balance and bliss.

Yet when the magical doctrines of Kabbalism came to ideological dominance in the 18th century, producing the so-called "Age of Enlightenment," they produced not the path to renewal of the earth and a return to Eden, but the imposition and reign of "the Satanic mills" of the industrial revolution and a foreshadowing of the subjugation of humanity by an esoteric elite by means of machine

---

[172]Ibid., pp. 39-40.

[173]The groundwork for the "repair" is rooted in government micro-management of our lives, along Talmudic lines of hair-splitting minutiae (cf. Gittin 4). Such unyielding bureaucracy paves the way for the apparatus of total control. Kabbalistic mysticism emerges as the antidote to control, in this dialectical process; cf. Rabbi Yitzchak Nissenbaum, *Derushim ve-Homer li Derush, Kinyanei Kedem, b-Reishit;* Rabbi Yitzhak ha-Kohen Kook, *Orot hakodesh* [Jerusalem: Mossad HaRav Kook, 1985].

surveillance and control. [174]

The dialectical process engendered by immersion in the Judaic ideology of redemption of the world produced a cataclysmic reversal, a "profound irony" missed by most of the historians of modern science. The supposed Kabbalistic philosophy of "harmony" espoused by Judaized, Gentile Renaissance occultists such as Pico, Reuchlin, Giorgio and Dee, led to the imposition of the tyranny of rationalism and materialism, in what Frances Yates terms a momentous shift from magic to mechanism:

"It is one of the more profound ironies of the history of thought that the growth of mechanical science, through which arose the idea of mechanism as a possible philosophy of nature, was itself an outcome of the Renaissance magical tradition. Mechanism divested of magic became the philosophy which was to oust Renaissance animism and to replace the 'conjuror' by the mechanical philosopher."[175]

In other words, once the principle of the religion of Judaism as expressed in the Kabbalah, of man's prideful, god-like power and his lofty "right" to tamper with Divine Creation, was established, and scientism began to emerge as a system of thinking and action unfettered by traditional restraints and fear of God, the mystical aspects of the philosophy were discarded, leaving Satanic pride to wed itself to technological prowess.

---

[174]"And was Jerusalem builded here, among those dark Satanic mills?" (William Blake, *Jerusalem,* 1810). The vulnerability of people to management, surveillance and control was exploited in the industrial age by political economist Jeremy Bentham whose Panopticon ("all-seeing") penal architecture has become a dominant metaphor among surveillance cognoscenti today.

[175]Yates, op. cit., p. 113. The pre-eminent "mechanical philosopher" symbolizing this shift was René Descartes, a product of the Jesuit college of La Fleche.

The Challenge to Christianity

It should be understood--though the fact that it even needs to be stated is itself a comment on our times--that this critical study of the religion of Judaism and its strange gods, Talmud, Kabbalah and self-worship, is not an attack on those people who call themselves or are regarded as Jewish today.

The greatest critic of Phariseeism was Jesus Christ. His criticism was an act of liberation for those who had "ears to hear." Scripture declares, "Thou shalt call His name Jesus for He shall save His people from their sins" (Matthew 1:21).

It is only the enemies of the Jewish people, including the religious heirs of the Pharisaic leadership today, who regard fidelity to Christ's mission as a hateful or an anti-Jewish act.

The religion of Judaism, the religion of Talmud and Kabbalah, is an all-encompassing form of totalitarianism. To expose tyranny is an act of emancipation.

Recall Talmud tractate Baba Mezia 59b in which a sly rabbi debates God and through trickery defeats Him. The Talmud has God admitting that the rabbi bested Him.

William N. Grimstad comments on this "unhealthy attitude of deception toward God himself...Since God can be so blithely duped, a similar attitude has spread toward other Jews--usually poorer ones....not to mention toward Gentiles." [176]

"The first Jewish dissenters from Judaism in modern times...became principled opponents of the religion that from their perspective tried to subject them to ...totalitarian controls." [177]

In the 17th century, when Baruch Spinoza rejected the Talmud and the Kabbalistic doctrine of Moses of Cordovero and began to study Christianity in earnest, the elders of the Amsterdam synagogue offered him a large pension "if he would consent to maintain at least an external loyalty

---

[176]Grimstad, op. cit., p. 256.

[177]Shahak and Mezvinsky, op. cit., p. 26.

to his synagogue and faith."

He refused.

In 1656, at age 24, he became the object of the local synagogue's cursing ceremony:

"...we anathematize, execrate, curse and cast out Baruch de Spinoza, the whole of the sacred community assenting, in the presence of the sacred books with the 613 precepts written therein...Let him be accursed by day, and accursed by night; let him be accursed in lying down and in rising up."

The threat of assassination was implicit in the curse and soon after, Spinoza was stabbed in the neck by a Jewish attacker wielding a dagger.

While there is a perpetual clamor nowadays in consequence of the ordeal of Anne Frank hiding from Nazis in an attic in Holland, the public know nothing of the Christian convert Spinoza hiding from the rabbis in an attic on the Outerdek road, outside of Amsterdam, shielded by Dutch Mennonites. [178]

In some quarters, particularly among the establishment media and American universities, one can only be certified as a good person if one gives aid and comfort not to the Spinozas of our time, but to their persecutors.

There is also pressure to impute to the New Testament charges of "hate," with inevitable calls for the suppression of the Gospel of John or Matthew, or, failing that, the deletion -- or distortion through dishonest translation -- of those passages which offend the religious heirs of the Pharisees today as much as they did 2000 years ago.

---

[178]Will Durant, *The Story of Philosophy* [NY: Time, Inc., 1962], pp. 139-148. The Chief Rabbi of Amsterdam in 1656 was Manesseh ben Israel, who inveigled Cromwell into admitting adherents of Judaism into England, from which they had been banished since 1290. The would-be assassins of Spinoza were thus welcomed into the Puritan Commonwealth, though not by unanimous consent. Some leading Puritans argued against the admission; cf. William Prynne, *A Short Demurrer to the Jewes Long Discontinued Remitter into England* [London: Edward Thomas, 1656].

In a 1995 speech at Hebrew University, Cardinal Joseph Bernardin of Chicago blamed the Gospel of John for "inciting anti-semitism."

He initiated a dialogue concerning the possible need for its redaction or suppression.

The rationale for censorship of certain "offensive" passages, or even the gradual phase-out of "obsolete" versions of the New Testament, such as the Douai-Rheims and King James, is the temporal chauvinist appeal to the phantasmagoria that due to the so-called "Holocaust,"[179] we have now entered a revolutionary new age, where we are duty-bound to scrutinize every traditional Western thought and action of the past 2,000 years in the light of whether or not these thoughts or actions may have contributed to making the "Holocaust" possible.

History, art, politics, culture and language itself are deemed worthy and legitimate solely by the degree to which they represent a panegyric to Judaism.

This sense of having entered a new order in relations with Jewish power and ideology has been brought about by the immense influence of the gargantuan, modern infotainment culture and "news" media network.

Through the unprecedented power of this network the record of the past has been warped by fanatical obsession and the millennia-old tapestry that is the history of the West has been reduced to a single criterion for determining decency and benevolence: "Was it good or bad for the

---

[179]From the Greek, *holokauston,* "wholly burnt," which is an apt description of the victims of Allied bombings in Hiroshima, Nagasaki and Dresden; and of the Israeli air force bombing of Lebanon in 1982, which killed 17,000 Arab civilians (cf. London *Evening Standard,* June 12, 2000). The devices employed to establish a proprietary relationship between Jews, martyrdom and the lexicon of anguish is a study in itself. Cf. Hoffman, "Jewspeak: A Critical Analysis of the Language of Mind Control," *Revisionist History,* No. 7 (1998); and Hoffman, "Psychology and Epistemology of 'Holocaust' Newspeak," *Journal of Historical Review,* Vol. 6, no. 4 (1986), pp. 467-478.

Jews?"[180]

The singular characteristic of the agenda of contemporary churchmen, presidents and prime ministers is this racial exceptionalism, which elevates obsequious concern -- bordering on idolatry -- for Jewish people above all other people. The ethnic supremacism of the Talmud and Kabbalah is perversely endorsed by Christian prelates and Gentile politicians who claim to be in the forefront of "combating racism."

Hence, it is said that Christian imprecations against the Jews and their rabbis through the ages have helped form the Nazis' anti-semitic animus, creating a "cultural framework" that made the "Holocaust" possible. The delirious milieu of "Holocaust" hysteria prescribes immunity from criticism for Jews, as epitomized by James Gerstenzang, staff writer for the *Los Angeles Times*, who opined that "public criticisms of Jews have historically been precursors to more organized attacks, and indeed were signals of the onslaught of the Nazi Holocaust." [181]

The *NY Times* says that to protest the crimes of the Israelis, "reeks of anti-semitism" because it "suggest(s) that survivors of the Holocaust are to be condemned for establishing a haven in the only state in which Jews form the majority." [182]

---

[180] One "replacement theology" that seems to have escaped attention, is the substitution of Auschwitz for Calvary as the greatest crime of all time. In terms of sacred status in the modern West, Auschwitz is many magnitudes above Calvary. Skeptics are prosecuted, fined and even imprisoned in Europe and Canada for "denying" Auschwitz gas chambers, as for example in France under the Fabius-Gayssot Act, enacted at the behest of the Chief Rabbi, René-Samuel Sirat. Needless to say, there are no civil or criminal penalties in any western nation for denying Calvary or mocking the Cross. In fact, in Poland Christians such as Kazimierz Switon have been arrested for defending the Cross (cf. *Jewish Chronicle,* March 3, 1999).

[181] LA Times, Feb. 6, 1990, p. A5.

[182] *NY Times,* Dec. 17, 1991, p. A20.

In both instances, protest and criticism that are perfectly acceptable with regard to any other people become a monstrous, stench-filled "precursor" to yet another "Holocaust" when directed at this special class, this officially-sanctioned Holy People who call themselves "Jews."

Meanwhile, high-level Jewish participation in the mass murder of twenty million Christians in Russia and Eastern Europe perpetrated by Jewish Communists such as Lenin, Trotsky, Zinoviev, Yagoda and Kaganovich, has unaccountably faded into a barely perceptible historical memory, even though it surpasses in duration, intensity and casualty figures the so-called "Holocaust." [183]

Journalist Joseph Sobran asks: "...might the Talmudic imprecations against Christ and Christians have helped form the Bolshevik Jews' anti-Christian animus? Did the Talmud help form the 'cultural framework' for the persecution of Christians, and for the eradication of Christian culture in America today? If so, will Jews make an effort to expunge the offending passages from the Talmud?...Where is the corresponding statement of Jewish leaders repudiating and repenting the Jewish role in a (Communist) cause?..." [184]

Purimspiel

As in all totalitarian systems, someone is always trying to get free of the ideological prison that is Judaism. Many sincerely desire an alternative to a life of hyper-regimentation, institutionalized criminality and destructive hatred.

By analyzing the hidden psychology of "Purimspiel" one discovers the means by which the Sanhedrin keeps Jewish people in subjection and enforces their obedience to stifling

---

[183]"By 1938 the Russian Orthodox Church was, for all intents and purposes crushed...with the annihilation of a large portion of the clergy" (M.V. Shkarovski, *Slavic Review,* Summer, 1995, p. 381).

[184]*Sobran's,* May 1999, p. 5.

Talmudic conformity and racial segregation. [185]

The spring festival of Purim *enshrines* the role of the hereditary oppressor (in this case Haman) as part of a function of keeping the Jewish people subservient to Judaism's religious and political overseers.

In the arcane Talmudic and Kabbalistic psychology (*Hester Panim*) of Purim,[186] a certain amount of violent persecution is regarded as desirable for maintaining the loyalty of the Jewish people to their duplicitous and corrupt leaders.

Without such anti-Jewish violence, the rabbis believe that Jewish people will wander from the rabbinic fold, marry a *shiksa* ("female abomination," i.e. a Gentile woman) and assimilate Gentile and Christian values, all of which are regarded as calamities.

The hidden aspect of Purim can be traced to the Talmudic command to get drunk on Purim (Megillah 7b). This injunction is an allusion to the revelation of a secret. The Talmud observes that "when wine goes in, secrets come out" (Eiruvin 65a).

The Kabbalistic understanding is that the Jew is to get intoxicated not on wine but on the secret within Purim itself, i.e., the conjunction of opposites, of Mordechai the Jew and Haman the exterminator of Jews, whose distinctions are blurred because *they both serve the purposes of Judaism.*[187]

Therefore, where no violent anti-Jewish persecution exists, the rabbis have found it necessary to foment and bankroll it, a fact perhaps unknown by those throughout

---

[185]For the remarkable story of how Jews established racial segregation in New York City, displacing Puerto Ricans and blacks, cf. George Kranzler, *Hasidic Williamsburg* [Northvale, NJ: Jacob Aronson, 1995], and Kit R. Roane, "New Neighbors Pushing at the Edge," *NY Times,* July 19, 1999.

[186]Chullin 139b.

[187]Also cf. Zohar Bereishis 36 and Zohar Chadis 2:137b.

history, such as Martin Luther,[188] as well as Hitler, among others, who advocated or implemented vigilante, military or other violence against non-criminal and non-combatant Jewish people. By so doing they only strengthened the stranglehold of the Jewish ruling class -- whether Zionist or rabbinic -- over the Jewish people. [189]

Although the supremacist character of both Judaism and Zionism cannot be gainsaid, we must acknowledge that there are numerous individuals described as "Jews" who embrace neither doctrine, and who are not engaged in any kind of anti-Christian or criminal activity. Moreover, even with regard to the arch-criminals who crucified Him, Jesus believed that it was sufficient to boldly speak the truth about them. Any other remedy was left to Divine Providence and due process of law (Romans 12:19 and 13:4).

---

[188]In his early career Luther had been an admirer of Konrad Muth, the leader of the *Mutianischer Bund* and the Kabbalistic secret society, *Obscurorum virorum* ("Obscure Men"). In 1514 Luther justified Judaism's resistance to Christendom, believing that only his reformed religion would prove attractive to multitudes of Jewish converts. (Cf. G. Lloyd Jones, *On the Art of the Kabbalah* [Lincoln, NE: Univ. of Nebraska, 1993], pp. 23-24). When the anticipated mass conversions failed to take place, the embittered reformer penned, "On the Jews and their Lies," [*Luther's Works,* Philadelphia: Fortress, 1971, v. 47]. This infamous, 1543 advocacy of arson and vandalism had no Scriptural warrant and has been rightly condemned. However, scant attention has been paid to Luther's 1525 pamphlet, *Against the Robbing and Murderous Hordes of Peasants,* in which he advised the rulers to "stab, strike and strangle" the "Satanic" German peasants. Luther's homicidal polemic against the peasantry was written in the same year that saw the slaughter of more than 6,000 peasant rebels in Thuringia, a pogrom that is seldom the focus of any outrage or commemoration. Luther's polemic against Jews was mild in comparison.

[189]Cf. Hoffman, "The Terror-Tricksters: Middle East Bombings and the Zionist Chess Game," *Independent History and Research Newsletter* (Spring, 1996, no. 4), pp. 8-10.

Today the heirs of the Pharisees are discerned not by racial or ethnic criteria but by a supremacist ideology. Judaism is a cabal of thought, not a cabal of race.

The famous statement in the book of Matthew about Christ's blood being on the children of the Jews has long since expired, for where today is there a racially pure "Jew" descended from the people of that era?[190]

But for a minuscule remnant, contemporary "Jews" are mostly *mamzerim*, of mixed race. A large segment of so-called Israeli "Jews" today are North African Sephardic people who are genetically indistinguishable from their Arab neighbors, while the overwhelming majority of "Jews" in America are actually descendants of converts from the Khazar tribe of Eastern Europe:

"After considering the strong evidence for cultural, linguistic and ethnic ties...one can only come to one conclusion: that the Eastern European Jews are descended from both the Khazars and other converts, as well as from Judeans...Ashkenazic Jews have the right, as well as the obligation, to rediscover and reclaim our unique, mixed heritage. Many of us are, indeed, heirs to the great Khazar Empire that once ruled the Russian steppes."[191]

The extent to which the mixed racial character of the people who call themselves Jews has been acknowledged, beneath Judaism's covert charade, by the rabbis themselves, is instructive. One manifestation of this awareness centers on the heavily shrouded inner teaching that the adherents of Judaism are racially descendants of Cain. The secret teaching of one school of the Kabbalah centers on the instruction of Rabbi Isaac Luria who emphasized the high status of Cain. Rabbi Luria taught

[190]Matthew 27: 24-25.

[191]Kevin Alan Brook, *The Jews of Khazaria* [Northvale, NJ: Jacob Aronson, 1999], p. 305-306. Brook's important study also contains a valuable section on the Karaites (pp. 296-299). Also cf. Paul Wexler, *The Ashkenazic Jews: A Slavo-Turkic People in Search of a Jewish Identity* [Columbus, Ohio: Slavica Publishers, 1993] and Arthur Koestler, *The Thirteenth Tribe: The Khazar Empire and Its Heritage* [NY: Random House, 1976].

that the spirit of Cain would increasingly prevail in the world as the realization of the process of *tikkun olam* is achieved: "...therefore, many of the great figures of Jewish history are represented as stemming from the root of Cain, and as the messianic time approaches, according to Isaac Luria, the number of such souls will increase."[192]

This is particularly perverse in light of the fact that Jewish lore holds that Cain is the literal descendant of Satan, conceived during sexual intercourse between Eve and the serpent.[193]

In spite of Rabbi Luria's diabolic fantasy, as Brook and other scholars have demonstrated, the overwhelming majority of people identified as Jewish have descent neither from Cain nor David.

They carry no racial taint or racial stigma. Whether they come under God's wrath or His blessing is decided by the choices they make as human beings possessed of the free will to choose good or evil.

To structure one's life according to the precepts of the Talmud and Kabbalah or its secular variants, Zionism and Communism, to adhere to the man-made traditions, pride and self-worship of Judaism, dooms the adherent to the enmity of God. Like all mankind, Jewish people can choose Christ or anti-Christ, truth or lies, freedom or bondage.

Anyone who sincerely wishes to be a true friend to an adherent of Judaism, will do as Jesus did: expose the Pharisaic system and expound the Gospel.

Only the enemies of the Jewish people, posing as friends in order to gain favor in the eyes of the world, would encourage people to remain in bondage to the rabbinic system that traps them as surely as it once trapped Paul.

---

[192]Gershom Scholem, op. cit., p. 163.

[193]Yevamot 103b. Also cf. Weiland (op. cit.).

Papal Treason Symbolizes General Apostasy

Journalist Robert K. Dahl says that Pope John Paul II's acquiescence to Judaism "has the appearance of treason, regardless of intent."[194] Indeed, in 1999, when John Paul II made the unprecedented decree that "the seeds infected with anti-Judaism" must "never again take root..." he was forbidding opposition to the religion of the Pharisees and proscribing the basis of the mission of Jesus Christ. [195]

Given the vast repository of documents, manuscripts, learned treatises and privileged correspondence pertaining to Judaism dating almost to the foundation of Christendom which are on deposit in the Vatican archives,[196] John Paul II cannot be speaking from ignorance when he claims, as he did in the synagogue of Rome, April 13, 1986 that "Jews are our elder brothers in the faith."[197]

Since adherents of the religion of Judaism do not have faith in either Jesus or the Old Testament law and prophets, but in the Talmudic and Kabbalistic traditions, exactly what faith is it that John Paul II shares with these *"elder brothers"* of his?

When this pope claimed that opposition to the religion of Judaism was opposition to the Old Testament, that the religion of Judaism is "a response to God's revelation in the Old Covenant" and that the "Eucharistic prayers" of Christian worship are "according to the models of Jewish

---

[194]*The Remnant,*[St. Paul, MN.], April 15, 1998.

[195]Statement of Pope John Paul II in his "General Audience" at Rome, April 28, 1999, as reported in the official Vatican newspaper, *L'Osservatore Romano*, May 5, 1999.

[196]On Feb. 27, 1994 a bomb was placed in the Maronite Catholic, Notre-Dame de La Delivrance Church, in Junieh, Lebanon, killing ten Catholics and wounding 60 others. The Vatican is aware of the fact that Lebanese Prime Minister Rafik al-Hariri and Interior Minister Michel Samaha indicated the massacre was engineered by Israeli intelligence. Cf. *NY Post,* Feb. 28, 1994.

[197]*L'Osservatore Romano*, English ed., April 21, 1986, p. 6.

tradition," he was either babbling dementia or falling far short of the truth. [198]

When, on Good Friday, 1998, the Pope turned the Christian Gospel upside down and proclaimed that "Jews have been crucified by us for so long," it was one of the most atrocious examples of modern Catholicism's slavishly Judaic orientation.

John Paul II is pretending that Judaism is the Old Testament faith minus Christ. But even if that false proposition were true, the Pharisaic *leadership* would still be guilty of deicide, as Thomas Aquinas held:

"The rulers of the Jews knew that He was the Messiah: and if there was any ignorance in them it was affected ignorance, which could not excuse them. Therefore their sin was the most grievous, both on account of the kind of sin as well as from the malice of their will." [199]

Moreover, the Bible itself declares unambiguously the guilt of the Jewish leadership and the fact that those who adhere to the dogma of these assassins are under wrath:

"For ye brethren became followers of the churches of God which in Judea are in Christ Jesus: for ye also have suffered like things of your own countrymen, even as they have of the Jews: who both killed the Lord Jesus and their own prophets and have persecuted us; and they please not God and are contrary to all men: forbidding us to speak to the Gentiles that they might be saved, to fill up their sins always: for the wrath is come upon them to the uttermost." (I Thessalonians 2:14-16).

No pope, preacher, president, prime minister, or professor has one scintilla of authority or competence to overthrow the preceding words. The whole world may be arrayed against the word of God but its force and validity endures.

The recent movement within the Church to declare opposition to Judaism an accursed form of "anti-semitic racism" is, in its inspiration and praxis, thoroughly

[198]"Jews and Christians Share Much Together," *L'Osservatore Romano,* English ed., May 5, 1999.

[199]*Summa Theologica,* Q. 47, Art. 6 Pt. III.

Talmudic, for it either extinguishes the New Testament's teachings or distorts them to such a degree that they are effectively made "of none effect."

This movement must also ignore or negate 2,000 years of historic Christian exposition of these teachings.

The extra-Biblical and anti-Christian nature of this fifth column within the Church is patent. It derives its credibility almost entirely from the blind allegiance it commands from Christians duped by usurpers and traitors occupying high ecclesiastical office, and by the tremendous glamor which the media accord it.

Since the great criterion of Jesus Christ for assessing the diabolic or the divine was "by their fruits ye shall know them," we discern that the fruits of today's Protestant and Catholic leaders are mostly rotten in this regard. As such, their actions reveal that they are neither "vicars of Christ," nor His ministers or saints. They are in fact agents of Judaism in all but name.

Therefore, the various anathemas these impostors and apostates thunder against Christians, whose only crime is to believe as all the apostles, martyrs and saints of the Church always did, has about the same moral authority as a pronouncement from the Secretary General of the U.N. or the Master of the Masonic Lodge. [200]

The hidden hand of Talmud and Kabbalah is revealed wherever the Jewish people are made the objects of veneration and sanctity. Jewish supremacy was opposed from the earliest days of the Church. John Chrysostom wrote: "Jesus said to them, 'If you are children of Abraham, do the works of Abraham, but as it is, you are seeking to kill me.' Here he repeatedly returned to their murderous design and reminded them of Abraham. He did this because He wanted to detach them from their racial pride and to deflate their excessive conceit, and to persuade them to no longer place their hope of salvation in Abraham or nobility

---

[200] Given that the occupation of even the highest of church offices is no longer a guarantor of fidelity to Jesus Christ, the question of who holds true Christian authority is one of the thorniest questions facing Christians today.

of race, for this was the thing that prevented them from coming to Christ; namely that they taught that the fact of their descent from Abraham sufficed for their salvation."[201]

By his radical departure from Biblical teaching and Christian practice, John Paul II and hundreds of thousands of Catholic and Protestant leaders who share his "elder brothers in the faith" falsehood, reveals himself as an accomplice of anti-Christ, by Scriptural definition: "Such a man is the anti-Christ who denies the Father and the Son. No one who denies the Son has the Father" (I John 2:23).

Christ testified that "no man cometh unto the Father except by me." Yet men have grown "dull of hearing" (Hebrews 5:11) and to the great drama of Christian salvation prefer instead a bland accommodation with the spirit of the modern age, which holds that a civilization based on the Father can be created by those who have made a religion out of denouncing and rejecting His Son.

This delusion, which would be laughable were its consequences not so tragic, has led to the rise of legions of "Judeo-Christians," who equate Judaism's strange gods with authentic Old Testament Israel and who go so far as to claim that it is necessary for Christians to embrace Judaism in order to be justified before God.

They look to a religion based on a Pharisaic sect comprised of the irreconcilable enemies of Christ for clues on how to become a better follower of Christ!

Worse, they intimate that Jesus is a liar. Jesus *directly* condemns the "tradition of the elders" and its "commandments of men," which are the oral basis of the idolized books, Talmud and Kabbalah. (Matthew 15:1-9, Mark 7:1-13).

Jesus puts paid to the lie that the Pharisees had any oral teaching from Moses. He tells them that if Moses were really their teacher they would follow Him (Jesus), not their tradition (John 5:46-47).

The brazen betrayal and hypocrisy of Judeo-Christians

[201]*The Fathers of the Church: St. John Chrysostom* [New York: Fathers of the Church, Inc., 1960), p. 70.

in the face of clear Gospel teaching on this subject, bids battle and defiance unto Heaven itself.

The glorified modern popes, preachers, politicians and rabbis often succeed for a time in deceiving the multitude, and in gathering a large and noisy following in this world, but their deeds also follow them and proclaim their evil, long after the paeans of media praise have wafted away on the sands of time. God is not mocked.

Glossary

Aggadah. "Discourse." Aggadah is a description of that portion of the rabbinic texts which concern miscellaneous folklore and tales of rabbis and their exploits, among other ephemera. In 1516, the Aggadot were collected by Rabbi Yaakov Ibn Chaviv and published as the *Ein Yaakov*.

Am-ha'aretz. "People of the Land." Derisive rabbinic term for the Israelite peasant farmers of Galilee of "simple faith," who tended to respect only Old Testament law, rather than the oral tradition, were lax about paying taxes to the rabbinate; did not eat and wash according to the ritual purity codes of the Pharisees, and from whom were drawn some of the first followers of Jesus. The Am-ha'aretz appear in John 7:46-49 where they are called "this people" and are cursed by the Pharisees because they "believe on him" (Christ) and "knoweth not" the (oral) "law."

Halakhah. "Law." The encyclopedic set of rabbinic rules that governs the lives of those who adhere to the religion of Judaism down to the smallest details of their existence, the ultimate source of which is the Talmud.

Kabbalah. ("Tradition received"). Major treatises on magic and demonology produced by rabbis from the second century A.D. onward, pertaining to the use of "protective" amulets and charms, the determination of lucky and unlucky days and numbers and numerical codes within words; reincarnation, spells and rituals; the doctrine of magical androgyny and the "rectification" of God's "imperfect Creation" through the redemptive capacity found only in the Jewish man. Two of the most prominent books of Kabbalah are the Sefer Yetzirah ("Book of Creation") and the Zohar ("Book of Splendor"), which runs to five volumes in the abridged Soncino translation.

With Judaism's prestige at an all-time high in the West, dozens of volumes of Kabbalah selections have been issued by major publishing houses with the demonology and racism excised, leaving only those portions that appeal to the appetite of New Age mystics for imaginary forays into realms of "bliss and harmony." These publishers are quite successful at profiting from the human capacity for endless self-deception.

Karaites. "Scripturalists." Derisive rabbinic term for anti-rabbinic "heretics" who studied the Old Testament scriptures independent of the Talmud. The Karaites came to prominence in the eighth century A.D. under the leadership of Anan ben David. The Karaites were expelled from Spain by Rabbi Joseph ben Faruj. In the Mishneh Torah (ch.10), Maimonides calls the Karaites "students of Tzadok" and decrees capital punishment for their "Bible only" stand.

Midrash. "To search out." A type of rabbinic literature composed mostly between 400 and 1200 A.D., featuring interpolations and fanciful emendations of Biblical texts. How tall was Adam? Midrash has the answer. What did Cain say to Abel? The Midrash supplies "the missing dialogue." For those curious about how people passed their time during the Flood, the always edifying Midrash informs us that Ham sodomized a dog on board Noah's Ark (Midrash Rabbah 1:292-293).

Mishnah. "Repetition." The first book of the Talmud, it constitutes a six part codification of the formerly oral "tradition of the elders." The Mishnah was written in a Middle Hebrew jargon and completed in Babylon toward the end of the second century A.D. It constitutes the basis of the laws (halakhah) of the religion of Judaism.

Mishnah Torah. "Repetition of the law." This 1180 A.D. codification of Talmudic law is the *magnum opus* of the highly influential Rabbi Moses Ibn Maimon, called by the acronym "Rambam," a.k.a. Moses Maimonides.

Shulhan Arukh. ("The Set Table"). An authoritative codification of Talmudic law by the Sephardic Rabbi Joseph Karo (1488-1575), edited circa 1565 by Polish Rabbi Moses Isserles to render it more appealing to Khazar adherents of Judaism.

Talmud. "Instruction." The Talmud is the Holy Writ of the religion of Judaism and constitutes the binding, formerly oral, tradition of the elders, committed to writing in Babylon toward the end of the second century A.D., forming the Mishnah.

Subsequent books of the Talmud were composed in Babylon as late as the sixth century A.D. and consist of explanations and illustrations of the Mishnah. There are also numerous later analyses of the exegesis, forming a vast compendium of super-fine, lawyerly distinctions. The Mishnah was written in a variant of Middle Hebrew. The later Talmudic books (Gemara) are written largely in Aramaic (sometimes called "Syriac" by the rabbis).

In addition to the Babylonian ("Bavli") Talmud, there is a Palestinian Talmud completed approximately 400 A.D. The Palestinian redaction does not have the influence or authority of the Babylonian version. The Talmud is traditionally studied aloud with a partner, accompanied by metronomic swaying.

The word Talmud has come to signify two different meanings. The first and preferred definition, as accepted by most lexicographers, denotes the books that comprise *both* the Mishnah and the Gemara as a whole. The second meaning connotes the Gemara alone, with the Mishnah standing apart as a separate textual entity.

The most recent English translation of the Talmud is the Steinsaltz edition from Random House (still in production as of this writing), which comprises 21 volumes to date.

The uncensored Talmud is replete with Procustean absurdities and the filthiest and most psychotic libels and maledictions aagainst non-Jews, women and Bible patriarchs conceivable. This writer has included but a small sample for purposes of documenting the authentic contents of this hate-canon. I have spared the reader numerous other Talmudic citations of sexual obsessions and pathologies so foul and despicable, they would be difficult for most people to even imagine. In spite of this, the Talmud should not be banned, since its unexpurgated contents are perhaps the greatest single indictment of the religion of Judaism. Maybe that is why, up until recently, the study of the complete and uncensored Talmud by Gentiles was an offense punishable by death (Sanhedrin 59a).

Books brimming with Talmud selections may be found in stores across the land, containing passages that have been falsified outright (as in the *Schindler's List* quotation), or carefully edited to restrict the contents only to those segments that can be construed as imparting the "wisdom and humanitarianism of the sages."

Tanakh. The books of the Hebrew Bible or more specifically, the Pentateuch, consisting of the first five books ("Humash").

Targum. An Aramaic version of the Tanakh translated by rabbinic partisans. It is typically published in a special edition known as the *Mikra'ot Gedolot,* in which only a small portion of the Targum appears in a thin margin, surrounded on the page by far lengthier teachings and commentary by "Rashi" (Rabbi Shlomo Itzhaki) and other rabbis.

Toledot Yeshu. A.k.a. Toledoth Jeshu.

Part of a genre of popular Jewish fables, this widely circulated rabbinic tale is a blasphemous pseudo-biography of Jesus, Mary and Joseph.

Torah.

References to the Torah in Judaism are invariably misleading. By dictionary definition, Torah denotes the books of the Old Testament (Tanakh). But in Judaism, the word Torah can signify the Talmud alone or both the Talmud and the Tanakh.

Tosefta.

"Supplement." Also based on the tradition of the elders, this minor work consists in material which the authors of the Mishnah chose not to include.

Yeshiva.

("Meeting"). Plural: Yeshiviot. A Talmud school for single men. Married men study Talmud in a *kollel*. It is considered a sign of high status to eschew work and study the Talmud for a lifetime. The Talmud school is characterized by shouting, disorder and vehement gesticulation. The "students" also eat, smoke and nap there.

Because the rabbinic "sages" regard Jewish women generally as "sacks of excrement" (Shabbat 152b), and "meat from a butcher shop" (Nedarim 20b), Talmud study for women is banned and Judaism makes no provision for Talmud schools for girls. This ban, which was decreed in Kiddushin 29b, has been upheld by the two most important codifiers of halakhah, Rambam and Karo.

Bibliography

Abed-Rabbo, Samir and Safie, Doris, eds. *The Palestinian Uprising* [Belmont, MA: AAUG, 1990].

Allis, Oswald, *Prophecy and the Church* [Philadelphia, 1945].

Aquinas, Thomas, *Summa Theologica* [Westminster, MD: Christian Classics, 1981], vol. 1-5.

Ashlag, Rabbi Yehuda L., *The Kabbalah: A Study of the Ten Luminous Emanations from Rabbi Isaac Luria* [Jerusalem: Research Centre of Kabbalah, 1974].

Assaf, Simha, *Ha-Onshin Aharei Hatimat ha-Talmud* ["Criminal Jurisdiction Since the Conclusion of the Talmud," Jerusalem, 1922].

Ball, George W. and Ball, Douglas, B., *The Passionate Attachment, America's Involvement with Israel, 1947 to the Present* [NY: W.W. Norton, 1992].

Ben-Yehuda, Nachman, *Political Assassinations by Jews* [Albany: State Univ. of NY Press, 1993].

Bialik, Hayyim and Ravnitzky, Yehoshua, eds., *The Book of Legends: Sefer-Ha-Aggadah* [NY: Schocken, 1992], trans. by Wm. G. Braude.

Blackman, Philip, trans., *The Mishnah* [NY: Judaica Press, 1964].

Bleefeld, Bradley, *Saving the Entire World And 100 Other Beloved Parables from the Talmud* [Plume, 1998].

Bleich, J. David, *Contemporary Halakhic Problems* [NY:KTAV, 1977].

Blumenfield, Samuel M., *Master of Troyes: A Study of Rashi the Educator* [NY: Behrman House, 1946].

Bokser, Ben Zion, *The Maharal: The Mystical Philosophy of Rabbi Judah Loew of Prague* [Northvale, NJ: Jacob Aronson,

1994].

Bokser, Ben Zion, *The Wisdom of the Talmud* [NY: Philosophical Library, 1951].

Brackman, Harold, 'The Ebb and Flow of Conflict: A History of Black-Jewish Relations through 1900" [1977 PhD. dissertation].

Buber, Martin, *Tales of the Hasidim* [NY: Schocken, 1948].

Buber, Solomon, ed., *Midrash Tanhuma* [Jerusalem: Ortsel Press, 1964].

Burton, Sir Richard Francis, *The Jew, the Gypsy and El Islam* [London, W.H. Wilkins, 1898].

Carmell, Aryeh, *Aids to Talmud Study* [NY: Feldheim Co., 1975].

Catholic Encyclopedia [NY: Robert Appleton, 1912].

Chrysostom, St. John, *Discourses Against Judaizing Christians* [Catholic Univ. of America Press, 1999], trans. by P.W. Harkins.

Chumatskyj, Yurij, *Why is One Holocaust Worth More than Others?* [Lidcombe, Australia, 1986].

Clifton, Tony and Leroy, Catherine, *God Cried* [London: Quartet Books, 1983].

Cohen, Abraham, *Everyman's Talmud: The Major Teachings of the Rabbinic Sages* [NY: Dutton, 1949].

Cooperman, Bernard, *Jewish Thought in the 16th Century* [Cambridge, MA: Harvard Univ. Press, 1983].

Cordovero, Moses, *Tomer Devorah* [London: Valentine & Mitchell, 1960], trans. by Louis Jacobs.

Crenshaw, Curtis I. and Gunn, Grover, *Dispensationalism Today, Yesterday and Tomorrow* [Memphis, TN: Footstool Publications, 1985].

Danby, Herbert, trans. *The Code of Maimonides* [New Haven,

CT: Yale Univ. Press, 1954].

Daube, David, *The New Testament and Rabbinic Judaism* [NY: Arno Press, 1973].

Davidy, Yair, *Lost Israelite Identity: The Hebrew Ancestry of the Celtic Races* [Jerusalem, Brit-Am, 1997].

Dilling, Elizabeth, *The Jewish Religion and Its Influence Today* [Torrance, CA: Noontide Press, 1983].

Dobin, Joel, *Kabbalistic Astrology: The Sacred Tradition of the Hebrew Sages* [Vermont: Inner Traditions, 1999].

Donin, Hayim, *To Be a Jew* [New York, 1991].

Dresner, Samuel, *The Zaddik* [NY: Schocken, 1974].

Durant, Will, *The Story of Philosophy* [NY: Time, Inc., 1962].

Edwardes, Allen, *Erotica Judaica* [NY: Julian Press, 1967].

Eisenberg, Robert, *Boychiks in the Hood: Travels in the Hasidic Underground* [NY: HarperCollins, 1995].

Elkins, Michael, *Forged in Fury* [NY: Ballantine Books, 1971].

Encyclopedia Judaica [Jerusalem: 1971].

Enziklopediya Talmudit [Jerusalem, 1947].

Epstein, I., et al., trans., *The Babylonian Talmud* [London: Soncino Press, 1935-1948], vol. 1-35.

Epstein, Jacob, *Introduction to the Text of the Mishna* [Jerusalem: Magnes Press, 1964].

Evola, Julius, *The Hermetic Tradition* [Vermont: Inner Traditions, 1994].

Fathers of the Church: St. John Chrysostom [New York: Fathers of the Church, Inc., 1960].

Fahey, Rev. Denis, *The Kingship of Christ and the Conversion of the Jewish Nation* [Regina Publications, 1953].

Fine, Lawrence, *Essential Papers on Kabbalah* [NY Univ. Press, 1995].

Finkelstein, Norman, *The Holocaust Industry: Reflections on the Exploitation of Jewish Suffering* [Verso Books, 2000].

Foxbrunner, Roman A., *Habad: The Hasidism of R. Shneur Zalman of Lyady* [Northvale, NJ: Jacob Aronson, 1993].

Frank, Yitzhak, *Practical Talmud Dictionary* [Philipp Feldheim, 1992].

Frankel, Yonah, *Readings in the Spiritual World of the Stories of the Aggada* [Tel Aviv: United Kibbutz Press, 1981].

Freedman, H. trans., *Midrash Rabbah* [London: Soncino Press, 1939], vol. 1-10.

Frieman, S., *Who's Who in the Talmud* [Northvale, NJ: Jacob Aronson, 1995].

Gastwirt, Harold, *Fraud, Corruption and Holiness: The Controversy Over the Supervision of the Jewish Dietary Practice* [NY: Kennikat Press, 1974].

Gedalia, Alon, *Toldot ha-Yehudim b'Eretz Yisroel be-Tekufat ha-Mishnah veha-Talmud* [Tel Aviv, 1952].

Gedalyahu, Alon, *Jews, Judaism and the Classical World: Studies in Jewish History in the Times of the Second Temple and Talmud* [Jerusalem: Magnes Press, 1977], trans. by Israel Abrahams.

Gelles, Benjamin, *Peshat and Derash in the Exegesis of Rashi* [EJ Brill: 1981].

Gibbon, Edward, *The Decline and Fall of the Roman Empire* [NY: Knopf, 1993], vol. 1-3.

Ginsburg, Yitzhak, et al., *Baruch Hagever* [Hebron: Kach, 1995].

Ginzberg, Louis, *Legends of the Jews* [Philadelphia: Jewish Publication Society, 1909-1939], vol. 1-7; trans. by Henrietta Szold et al.

Glatzer, Nahum, *Hillel the Elder* [NY: Schocken, 1966].

Goldberg, H.E., ed., *Judaism Viewed from Within and Without* [NY: State Univ. NY Press, 1986].

Gordon, Mary, *The Shadow Man* [NY: Random House, 1996].

Goshen-Gottstein, Alon, *The Body as Image of God in Rabbinic Literature* [Berkeley, 1991].

Grimstad, William N., *AntiZion* [Torrance, CA: Noontide Press, 1973].

Grimstad, William N., *Talk About Hate* [Colorado Springs, Colorado: Council on Hate Crime, 1999].

Grimstad, William N., *The Six Million Reconsidered* [Media Research Associates, 1977].

Gutman, G. et al., *Spice of Torah: Gematria* [Judaica Press, 1998].

Habib, Jacob ben Solomon, *Ein Yaakov: The Ethical and Inspirational Teachings of the Talmud* [Northvale, NJ: Jacob Aronson, 1999].

Halevi, Rabbi Yehuda, *The Kuzari* [Northvale, NJ: Jacob Aronson, 1998], N. Daniel Korobkin, trans.

Halivni, David, *Midrash, Mishnah and Gemara* [Cambridge, MA: Harvard Univ. Press, 1986].

Halsell, Grace, *Prophecy and Politics* [Westport, CT: Lawrence Hill & Co., 1986].

Handelman, Susan, *The Slayers of Moses: The Emergence of Rabbinic Interpretation* [Albany: State Univ. of NY Press, 1982].

Heilman, Samuel, *Defenders of the Faith: Inside Ultra-Orthodox*

Jewry [NY: Schocken, 1992].

Heinemann, Joseph, *The Literature of the Synagogue* [NY: Behrman House, 1975].

Heller, Joseph, *The Stern Gang* [Cass, 1995].

Helmreich, William, *The World of the Yeshiva* [NY: Free Press, 1982].

Himelstein, Shmuel, *The Jewish Primer* [Jerusalem: The Jerusalem Publishing House, 1990].

Hirschfeld, Hartwig, *Literary History of Hebrew Grammarians and Lexicographers* [London: Oxford Univ. Press, 1926].

Hoffman, Edward, *Against All Odds: The Story of Lubavitch* [NY: Simon & Schuster, 1991].

Hoffman, Michael A., *The Great Holocaust Trial* [Torrance, CA: Institute for Historical Review, 1985].

Hoffman, Michael A., *Secret Societies and Psychological Warfare* [NY: Wiswell Ruffin House, 1992].

Holtz, Barry, ed., *Back to the Sources: Reading the Classic Jewish Texts* [NY: Simon and Schuster, 1984].

Holy Bible, Douay-Rheims Edition [NY: P.J. Kennedy & Sons, 1914].

Holy Bible, King James Version: 1611 Edition [Nashville: Thomas Nelson, 1982].

Huppert, Uri, *Back to the Ghetto* [NY: Prometheus Books, 1988].

Idel, Moshe, *Golem: Jewish Magical & Mystical Traditions* [Albany: State Univ. of NY Press, 1990].

Idelsohn, Abraham, *The Ceremonies of Judaism* [Cincinnati: Nat'l Federation of Temple Brotherhoods, 1930].

Jacobs, Louis, *Jewish Mystical Testimonies* [NY: Schocken, 1977].

Jacobs, Louis, *Studies in Talmudic Logic and Methodology* [London: Valentine & Mitchell, 1961].

Jansen, Michael, *The Battle of Beirut* [Boston: South End Press, 1983].

Jonas, Hans, *The Gnostic Religion* [Boston: Beacon Press, 1963].

Jones, Vendyl, *Will the Real Jesus Please Stand?* [Tyler, TX: Institute of Judaic-Christian Research, 1983].

Jurgens, W.A., trans., *The Faith of the Early Fathers* [Collegeville, MN:Liturgical Press]. Vol. 1-3.

Kahan, Stuart, *The Wolf of the Kremlin: The First Biography of L.M. Kaganovich* [NY: Wm. Morrow, 1987].

Kaplan, Aryeh, trans., *Bahir* [York, ME: Samuel Weiser, 1990].

Kaplan, Aryeh, *Maimonides Principles* [Union of Orthodox Jewish Congregations of America].

Kaplan, Aryeh, trans., *Sefer Yetzirah* [York, ME: Samuel Weiser, 1997].

Katz, Jacob, *The Shabbos Goy* [Philadelphia, Jewish Publication Society, 1989], trans. by Yoel Lerner.

Katz, Michael and Schwartz, Gershon, *Swimming in a Sea of Talmud: Lessons for Everyday Living* [Jewish Pub. Society, 1998].

Kaye, Evelyn, *The Hole in the Sheet: A Modern Woman Looks at Orthodox and Hasidic Judaism* [Seacaucus, NJ: Lyle Stuart, 1987].

Kiener, Ronald, et al., *The Early Kabbalah* [Paulist Press, 1986].

Kimball, William, *The Rapture: A Question of Timing* [Grand Rapids, MI: Baker, 1985].

Kimball, William, *What the Bible Says About the Great Tribulation* [Phillipsburg, NJ: 1983].

Klein, Isaac, *A Guide to Jewish Religious Practice* [NY: Jewish Theological Seminary of America, 1979].

Koestler, Arthur, *The Thirteenth Tribe: The Khazar Empire and Its Heritage* [NY: Random House, 1976].

Kraemer, David, *The Mind of the Talmud* [NY: Oxford Univ. Press, 1990].

Krakovsky, Rabbi Levi Isaac, *Kabbalah: The Light of Redemption* [Jerusalem: Yeshivat Kol Yehuda, 1970].

Kranzler, George, *Hasidic Williamsburg* [Northvale, NJ: Jacob Aronson, 1995].

Lamm, Norman, ed., *The Religious Thought of Hasidism: Text and Commentary* [KTAV Publishing, 1999].

Landesman, Dovid, et al., *As the Rabbis Taught: Studies in the Aggados of the Talmud* [Northvale, NJ: Jacob Aronson, 1996].

Langer, Jiri, *Nine Gates to the Chassidic Mysteries* [NY:Behrman House, 1961].

Landau, David, *Piety and Power: The World of Jewish Fundamentalism* [NY: Hill and Wang, 1993].

Levi, Eliphas, *Transcendental Magic* [Middlesex, UK: Tiger Books, 1995], trans. by Arthur E. Waite.

Levy, Amnin, *The Haredim* [Jerusalem: Keter Publishing, 1989].

Lindemann, Albert S., *Esau's Tears: Modern Anti-Semitism and the Rise of the Jews* [NY: Cambridge Univ. Press, 1997].

MacLennan, Robert, *Early Christian Texts on Jews and Judaism* [Atlanta: Scholars Press, 1990].

MacPherson, Dave, *The Rapture Plot* [Simpsonville, SC: Millennium III Publishers, 1995].

McKee, Alexander, *Dresden 1945* [NY: Dutton, 1984].

Mahler, Raphael, *A History of Modern Jewry* [London: 1971].

Maimonides, Moses, *Mishnah Torah* [Brooklyn: Moznaim Publishing, 1990].

Maimonides, Moses, *The Guide of the Perplexed* [Chicago: Univ. of Chicago Press, 1963], trans. by Shlomo Pines.

Martin, Rev. Malachi, *The New Castle* [NY: Dutton, 1974].

Matt, Daniel, trans., *Zohar: The Book of Enlightenment* [Paulist Press, 1983].

Mayer, Arno, *Why Did the Heavens Not Darken? The "Final Solution" in History* [NY: Pantheon, 1988].

Mendelssohn, Moses, *Jerusalem, or On Religious Power and Judaism* [London, 1983], trans. by Allan Arkush.

Minerbi, Sergio, I., *The Vatican and Zionism,* [NY: Oxford Univ. Press, 1990].

Mordechai, Avi ben, *Signs in the Heavens: A Jewish Messianic Perspective of the Last Days & Coming Millennium* [Millennium 7000 Communications, 1996].

Myslobodsky, Michael S., *The Mythomanias: The Nature of Deception and Self-Deception* [Mahwah, NJ: Lawrence Erlbaum, 1997].

Neusner, Jacob, trans., *The Mishnah* [New Haven, CT: Yale Univ. Press, 1988].

Neusner, Jacob, *Rabbinic Judaism: Structure and System* [Minneapolis, MN: Augsburg Fortress, 1995].

Novick, Peter, *The Holocaust in American Life* [Boston: Houghton-Mifflin, 1999].

Otten, Herman, ed., *The Christian News Encyclopedia* [New Haven, Missouri, 1988].

Ouaknin, Marc-Alain, *The Burnt Book* [NY: Princeton Univ. Press, 1998], trans. by Llewellyn Brown.

Peters, Peter J., *Baal Worship* [LaPorte, Colo: Scriptures for America, 1995].

Pike, Theodore Winston, *Israel: Our Duty, Our Dilemma* [Oregon City, Oregon: Big Sky Press, 1984].

Plaut, Gunther W., *The Magen David* [B'nai B'rith Books, 1991].

Popper, William, *The Censorship of Hebrew Books* [Judaica Series, no. 6].

Pranaitis, J. B., *The Talmud Unmasked* [St. Petersburg, Russia: Imperial Academy of Sciences, 1892].

Provan, Charles D., *The Church is Israel Now* [Vallecito, Calif: Ross House Books, 1987].

Prynne, William, *A Short Demurrer to the Jewes Long Discontinued Remitter into England* [London: Edward Thomas, 1656].

Reed, Douglas, *The Controversy of Zion* [Bullsbrook, Australia: Veritas, 1985].

Restoration of the Original Sacred Name Bible [Winfield, Alabama: Missionary Dispensary Bible Research, 1977].

Reuchlin, Johann, *On the Art of the Kabbalah* [Lincoln, NE: Univ. of Nebraska Press, 1993], trans. by Martin Goodman.

Roberts, Alexander, et al., *Ante-Nicene Fathers* [Hendrickson Publishers, 1996], vol. 1-10.

Rops-Daniel, *Jesus and His Times* [Garden City, NY: Image Books, 1958].

Rosenbloom, Joseph, *Conversion to Judaism* [Cincinnati: Hebrew Union College Press, 1978].

Rosenberg, Roy A., *The Anatomy of God* [NY: KTAV, 1973].

Ruderman, David B., *Kabbalah, Magic and Science* [Cambridge, MA: Harvard Univ. Press, 1988].

Schlissel, Steve, and Brown, David, *Hal Lindsey & the Restoration of the Jews* [Edmonton, Canada: Still Waters Revival Books, 1990].

Scholem, Gershom, *Kabbalah* [Jerusalem: Keter Publishing House, 1974; reprinted 1978, New American Library].

Scholem, Gershom, et al., *Origins of the Kabbalah* [Philadelphia, Jewish Publication Society, 1987].

Scholem, Gershom, trans., *Zohar: The Book of Splendor* [NY: Schocken, 1963].

Secret Relationship Between Blacks and Jews [Boston: Historical Research, 1991].

Shahak, Israel, *Jewish History, Jewish Religion* [London: Pluto Press, 1994].

Shahak, Israel and Mezvinsky, Norton, *Jewish Fundamentalism in Israel* [London: Pluto Press, 1999].

Shapiro, James, *Oberammergau* [Little, Brown, 2000].

Shapiro, Michael, *The Jewish Hundred* [Secaucus, NJ: Carol Publishing, 1996].

Shereshevsky, Esra, *Rashi: The Man and His World* [NY: Sepher-Hermon Press, 1982].

Shilhav, Yosef et al., *Growth and Segregation: The Ultra-Orthodox Community of Jerusalem* [Jerusalem: Jerusalem Institute for Israeli Studies, 1986].

Shulman, Y. David, *The Chambers of the Palace: Teachings of Rabbi Nachman of Bratslav* [Northvale, NJ: Jason Aronson, 1993].

Soloveitchik, Joseph, *The Halakhic Mind* [NY: Free Press, 1986].

Sperber, Daniel, *Magic and Folklore in Rabbinic Literature* [Gefen Books, 1996].

Sperling, Harry, and Simon, Maurice, trans., *The Zohar* [London: Soncino Press, 1931-1934], vol. 1-5.

Staub, Jacob J., *The Creation of the World According to Gersonides* [Chico, Calif: Scholar's Press, 1982].

Steinsaltz, Adin, trans., *The Talmud: The Steinsaltz Edition* [New York: Random House, 1990-2000], vol. 1-21.

Steinsaltz, Adin, *The Essential Talmud* [NY Basic Books, 1976].

Stirling, William, *The Canon: An Exposition of the Pagan Mystery Perpetrated in the Cabala* [York, ME: Samuel Weiser, 1999].

Stone, Michael, ed., *Jewish Writings of the Second Temple Period* [Fortress Press, 1984].

Suares, Carlo, *The Cipher of Genesis: The Original Code of the Qabala as Applied to the Scriptures* [York, ME: Samuel Weiser, 1992].

Tannous, Izzat, *The Palestinians* [NY: LGT Co., 1988].

Tishbi, Yesaiah, *Torat ha-Rave-ha-Kelippah be-Kabbalat ha-Ari* ["The Theory of Evil and the Satanic Sphere in Kabbalah," Jerusalem: 1942; reprinted 1982].

Tresner, Jim, *Albert Pike: The Man Behind the Monument* [NY: M. Evans, 1995].

Twersky, Isadore, *Introduction to the Code of Maimonides* [New Haven, CT: Yale Univ. Press, 1980].

Urbach, Ephraim, *The Sages: Their Concepts and Beliefs* [Cambridge, MA: Harvard Univ. Press, 1987].

Unterman, Alan, *Dictionary of Jewish Lore and Legend* [London: Thames & Hudson, 1991].

Unterman, Isaac, *The Talmud: An Analytical Guide to Its History and Teachings* [Bloch Publishing, 1997].

Vital, Chayyim ben Joseph, *The Tree of Life: Chayyim Vital's Introduction to the Kabbalah of Isaac Luria - The Palace of Adam Kadmon* [Northvale, NJ: Jacob Aronson, 1999], trans. by D.W. Menzi and Zwe Padeh.

Volkogonov, Dimitri, *Lenin: A New Biography* [NY: Free Press, 1994].

Walsh, William Thomas, *Isabella of Spain* [Rockford, IL: Tan Books, 1987].

Wegner, Judith, *Chattel or Person? The Status of Women in the Mishnah* [NY: Oxford Univ. Press, 1988].

Weisfeld, Abie, *Sabra & Shatila: A New Auschwitz* [Jerusalem Publishing House, 1984].

Weiland, Ted, *Eve: Did She or Didn't She?* [Scottsbluff, NE: Mission to Israel, 2000].

Wiesel, Elie, *Souls on Fire: Portraits and Legends of Hasidic Masters* [NY: Random House, 1972].

Werblowsky, R.J.Z, *Joseph Karo* [Oxford, England: Oxford Univ. Press, 1962].

Wexler, Paul, *The Ashkenazic Jews: A Slavo-Turkic People in Search of a Jewish Identity* [Columbus, OH: Slavica, 1993].

Wexler, Paul, *The Non-Jewish Origins of the Sephardic Jews* [Albany: State Univ. of NY Press, 1996].

White, James and Sproul, R.C., *Sola Scriptura* [Soli Deo Gloria Publications, 1998]

Witness of War Crimes in Lebanon: Testimony Given to the Nordic Commission, Oslo [London, EAFORD/Ithaca Books, 1983].

Wright, William, *The Homilies of Aphraates, the Persian Sage* [London, 1869].

Yamahata, Yosuke, *Nagasaki Journey* [San Francisco: Pomegranate Artbooks, 1995].

Yates, Frances A., *The Occult Philosophy in the Elizabethan Age* [London: Routledge & Keegan Paul, 1979].

Yates, Frances A., *The Rosicrucian Enlightenment* [UK: Ark Paperbacks, 1986].

Zolli, Eugenio Israel, *Before the Dawn* [Ft. Collins, CO: Roman Catholic Books, 1997].

Zolli, Eugenio Israel, *The Nazarene* [Ft. Collins, CO: Roman Catholic Books].

Index

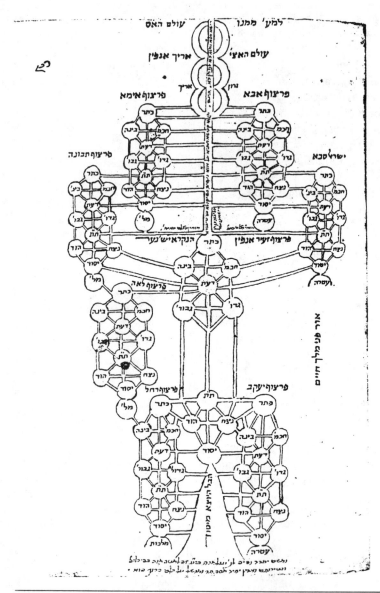

The structure of the *sefirot* (spirit emanations) according to the Kabbalah of "the great Ari," Rabbi Isaac Luria (1534-1572).